July 22, 2004

To Chad,

with appreciation for your dedication to remembering "our boys".

Sandra Bonella Thompson

Love, Honor, and Cherish

A True World War II Story of A Screaming Eagle and a Courageous Woman

Sandra Bonilla Thompson

Airborne Books • Savannah, Georgia

Airborne Books
118 Barnard Street
Box 8786
Savannah, Georgia 31401

Designed by Joe Loehle, Crawdad Studio, St. Simons Island, GA
Printed in the United States of America

Library of Congress Cataloguing in Publication Data

Thompson, Sandra Bonilla
Love, Honor, and Cherish: A True World War II Story of a Screaming Eagle and a Courageous Woman

ISBN 0-9749740-05

For John and Louise Keith,

Pearl and Emmett Hill, Dorothy Conaway, James and Florence Keith, Fred and Lois Keith, Claude Keith, Clyde Keith, all the cousins and their children and grandchildren, for Opal and Nicky, and with abiding love for Dena and Jeff Kemp and their sons Nicholas and Christopher

Table of Contents

Acknowledgements

I thank my father and mother for showing me that love never fails. I thank all veterans of World War II, in service and on the home front, for their devotion to their country. I thank my mother for saving more than five hundred letters, two thousand pages, and giving me permission to edit and publish them. I am indebted to family members who answered numerous questions about their experiences during the war and provided photographs for this book.

Carl Storch provided help with copying and cataloguing original documents. Clyde Taylor invited me to tell my parents' story to the Saint Simons Island Rotary Club, and I produced the first thirty-eight pages of this manuscript as a result. Hagan Thompson edited my earliest drafts. Joyce Pair assisted with editing, formatting and proofreading. Antje Maurel read an early manuscript and made excellent suggestions for change. Chuck Dowdy, Bob Pauxtis, and Bill Van Loan suggested including narratives of significant events of the war. Col. Jerry D. Autry, USA, Retired, and Mark Bando read the history of the 101st Airborne Division, 502nd Parachute Infantry Regiment and helped me correct errors. Any remaining errors are mine. My father's friend, Renaldo Angelini, read page proofs and gave me much encouragement. Thanks to Brenda English who edited and proofread my final draft.

I found moving descriptions of events of World War II in articles from the *Birmingham News* and *Birmingham Post* which my mother had saved. Material from these and other newspapers is credited in the text.

I told my family's story by reconstructing the letters my mother preserved and researching and summarizing events in the periods not covered by the letters. Reconstruction of the letters was necessary: they are brittle, and parts have crumbled away. Insects and mice destroyed pages. Ink transferred, creating double images on both sides of a page. Letters were undated, parts of letters were written at different times of day and on different dates, and dates on letters were different from dates of postmarks. V-mail letters, pages 4 1/2 inches wide by 5 1/2 inches long with a 1-inch header for the address, were difficult to read.

I edited the letters for grammar and punctuation, but I retained some non-standard grammatical usages to preserve the voices of my parents. Order of paragraphs in a letter, order of sentences in a paragraph, and order of words in a sentence may have been changed. Words have been added for clarity.

Chapter One

A Whirlwind Romance

AUGUST 1942

When Opal met Nicky in June 1942, she had been dating a man nicknamed Elmo. Elmo cared for Opal deeply, and he respected her family. Opal cared for Elmo, but she was not in love with him, and she had not considered marrying him.

Opal was attracted to Nicky more than she had ever been attracted to a man. He was handsome, confident, experienced, and greatly attracted to her. After dating Nicky for a few weekends, Opal stopped dating Elmo. Elmo was hurt and angry that Opal had rejected him for a soldier whom she had met only recently. Elmo told Opal that he hoped "the-son-of a-bitch [would be] killed in the war." The remark ended Elmo and Opal's friendship.

Soon, Nicky asked Opal to marry him, and within a few weeks, she accepted his proposal. They dated every weekend, but wrote few letters until the end of August.

★ ★ ★ ★ ★ ★ ★ ★ ★ ★ ★ ★ ★

August 25, 1942
Dear Opal,

I arrived safe but sleepy in Ft Benning. As I rode toward camp, I thought of you. You're a lovely girl, and I have a wonderful time with you. I will see you again Saturday night, and we'll go out to dinner.

Here's a sad story. The other day, a soldier came out to the field in a jeep and told me that Butch, my English bulldog, was hurt. I rushed back to camp, and I never saw such a pitiful sight. The dog was bleeding from the mouth, and his leg was hurt. Butch broke his leash and a mule kicked him in the face. I was mad. My men were standing around like a bunch of dopes. I borrowed a car and rushed Butch to town to the vet. The vet says Butch has a 50/50 chance. I told the vet to do everything he could for the poor dog.

When I come Saturday, I'm bringing your little wings. They will be a symbol of our engagement until I can buy a ring. And I have a surprise for you.
Always thinking of you,
Nicky

P. S. Pardon the stationery, but I don't care for fancy stationery. Do you? Here's a poem I wrote.

Beauty in the Restaurant

At the Paradise, they rave about their beauties,
At the Hollywood, they're nuts about their cuties;
Yet of one girl, I'm glad to boast a bit.
She has beauty, charm, and wit. She has IT.
The Casino has the lovely Mary Astor.
She'll make your heart beat a little faster.
But there's one who tops them all;
There's one who'll make you fall;
She's Opal, the most beautiful gem of all.

August 27, 1942
[This letter was typed, probably by Georgette Seals who lived in Opal's apartment house. Opal was self-conscious about her handwriting, but she could not type, and she did not own a typewriter.]
Dear Nicky,
I was very glad to receive your letter, but I was surprised. Since you are coming to Birmingham this weekend, I didn't expect you to write. I'm sorry about Butch, and I hope he'll recover. Poor li'l fellow. I hate mules anyway, and now I have another grudge against them.
You say you have a surprise for me. I've never cared for surprises, but perhaps this one will be different from the ones I've had before.
I enjoy seeing you and I am sure the weekend will be more pleasant because you will be here.
Sincerely,
Opal

September 1, 1942
Dear Opal,
You say you were surprised to receive my letter. I did promise to write, didn't I? Butch is home, but he is a changed dog. If anyone tries to pet him, he growls and snaps. Maybe he'll be more friendly when he gets well.
Sunday night when I left, I caught a special bus to Columbus *[Georgia]*. I got to the city at 1:30 A.M. Good time, don't you think?

Opal Keith

When I first saw you, my heart skipped a beat, and the more I see you, the more I care for you. But I know I'll have to make you care for me. Well, that's just what I'll do. Darling, I said I cared for Ann [a former girl friend], but it was just an infatuation.

I am going to New York next week. I wish you would go with me. I'd love to show you the sights, take you to a nice restaurant, and to a show on Broadway. I want to tell my family about us, but I'll wait until you're sure.

My leave starts Monday, but I may be able to get away Friday night if I don't get hurt when we jump tomorrow. If I don't see you Friday night, then I'll see you Saturday night.

Always,
Nicky

502nd Parachute Infantry Regiment

Nicky's outfit had been formed to challenge the might of Hitler's war machine. The Allies were stunned on May 10, 1940, when German paratroopers jumped deep into Holland and captured roads and bridges far behind front lines. Then, artillery and panzer divisions crushed Dutch defenses. In response, the U.S. Army developed a test parachute platoon in 1940 with Lt. Col. William C. Lee as commander. After Lt. Col. Lee studied the parachute towers at the New York World's Fair, (Nicky may have seen them there.) he moved his men to Hightstown, New Jersey, home of the Safe Parachute Company. While the test platoon trained in New Jersey, Lt. Col. Lee ordered four parachute towers for the Parachute School at Fort Benning.

The 502nd Parachute Battalion, activated in July 1941, became a Parachute Regiment in March 1942. On March 7, Col. Lee addressed the men of the new regiment.

> Officers and men of the 503rd and 502nd Parachute Regiments, this is a memorable day for American Parachute Troops. You are grouped for the first time into regiments. We shall not forget the 501st, the 502nd, and the 504th Parachute Battalions, for these units were the pioneers, the ones which made these regiments possible. Today these units exist no more as separate battalions. Instead, you have a larger and more powerful unit; one which increases your fighting and staying power; and one which magnifies your chances of success in battle....
>
> May the presentation of these Colors today kindle even higher our devotion to our country and inspire in each of us a grim determination to endure the hardships of the future, PROUD AND UNAFRAID *[sic]*. This is the spirit which in the end will bring us to victory. [2]

Paratrooper training towers at Fort Benning

Paratrooper training was difficult and dangerous. Parachute basic consisted of thirteen weeks of physical training, parachute packing, jump commands, parachute manipulation and landing, controlled descents from a tower, and five jumps from an airplane in flight (or as troopers said, "in fright") with one jump made at night. At Fort Benning on April 17, 1942, shortly before he met Opal, Nicky became a Qualified Parachutist.

Fort Benning

Fort Benning is set among rolling hills, pine forests, and tangled honeysuckle, blackberries and kudzu in western Georgia. Creek Indians settled the area, hunting, fishing, and raising crops until 1825, when William McIntosh, son of an American Revolutionary War hero and a Creek woman, ceded Creek land rights to the U.S. In exchange, McIntosh received a large plantation on the Chattahoochee River.

The fort was named for General Henry Lewis Benning, who recruited and led the 17th Georgia Volunteers during the Civil War. The military complex housed the Infantry School of Arms, which produced soldiers such as World War II Generals Omar Bradley, Dwight Eisenhower, George Marshall, and George Patton.

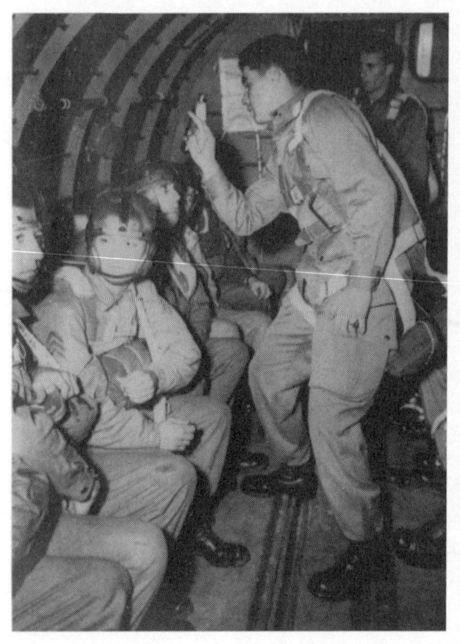

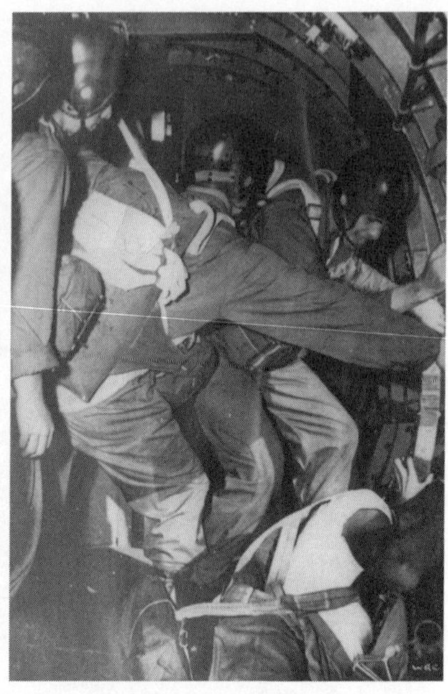

Paratroopers flying to drop zone and standing in the door wearing early Riddell headgear.

Across the Chattahoochee River in Alabama, airborne troops trained. The land was so hot and flat those troopers called it "the frying pan." Pvt. Marie McMillin, the world's champion woman parachute jumper, was chief of a section of riggers at the Parachute School; she was not eligible for paratrooper training.

Fort Benning bordered the city of Columbus, Georgia, and across the Alabama state line was Phenix City, a place notorious for vice of every kind. In 1953, Albert Patterson won the Democratic nomination for Attorney General of Alabama with a promise to clean up vice in Phenix City. He was murdered before the general election.

About forty miles away in Tuskegee, Alabama, a select group of African-Americans began pilot training. They would become known as the Tuskegee Airmen. Mrs. Eleanor Roosevelt flew with the African-American aviators to demonstrate her confidence in their piloting skills.

Soldiers from Fort Benning traveled regularly to Birmingham for a sample of city life. Paratroopers of the 502nd fielded a baseball team to compete with teams sponsored by the Tennessee Coal and Iron Company and other Birmingham industries.

The 101st Airborne Division was activated in August, and the 502nd was assigned to the new division. General William C. Lee took charge of the 101st. On August 17, he spoke to the men of the unit:

> The 101st . . . has no history, but it has a rendezvous with destiny. Like the early American pioneers whose invincible courage was the foundation stone of this nation, we have broken with the past and its traditions to establish our claim to the future. Due to the nature of our armament and the tactics in which we shall perfect ourselves, we shall be called upon to carry out operations of far-reaching military importance, and we shall habitually go into action when the need is immediate and extreme. [3]

The 502nd moved from Fort Benning, Georgia, to Fort Bragg, North Carolina, in September 1942.

★ ★ ★ ★ ★ ★ ★ ★ ★ ★ ★ ★ ★

September 20, 1942
Dear Opal,

This is probably the worst news I've heard in a long time. The 502nd is leaving Fort Benning. I don't know where we're going. We may go across [the Atlantic Ocean], or we may go to another camp. I hate to leave you, but I can't desert. I can't be a coward and a fool.

So I'm coming to Birmingham to marry you. If I can't come, I'll send for you. I want to spend every minute I can with you. I am sad and blue. Tears are in my eyes. I would never tell that to anyone but you. You are the one I love.

Always,
Nicky

September 23, 1942
Dear Opal,

This is the last letter I'll write you from Ft. Benning. We're leaving at 11: 00 A.M. When I reach my station, I'll write or send a telegram. Let's get married as soon as we can, and you can join me, wherever I am. I will be lonely without you, especially on Saturdays and Sundays.

By the way, Darling, I didn't get an extension on the furlough. The company commander sent a telegram to my home in New York saying come back quick, but I was in Alabama with you. The Captain said he will take care of me when we get to our new camp.

I may go to the end of the world, but I'll never be far from you.

Love always,
Nicky

September 24, 1942
Darling Nicky,

The news that you are leaving Fort Benning makes me sad and afraid. But you can depend on me to be brave and patriotic and keep a calm nerve. No matter where you go, I'll love you, and I'll be true.

Waiting 'til I see you again,
Opal

FORT BRAGG

Soon Nicky learned that his outfit would be training at Fort Bragg in the pine barrens of North Carolina. Rich planters bought flat coastal land for cotton, rice, and indigo plantations, and Scots and Irish immigrants settled in the uplands. Amid the small farms of the area, Camp Bragg was established in 1918 as a training facility for Field Artillery. The camp was named for Civil War General Braxton Bragg, a North Carolina native, a graduate of West Point, an Indian fighter, and a Lieutenant Colonel during the Mexican War. At Camp Bragg, soldiers learned to use artillery in sand, mud, streams, and forests. The camp became Fort Bragg in 1922.

During World War II, Fort Bragg had a population of 159,000 personnel, and as many as 1,000 new recruits were processed in a day. Among the gently rolling hills, the newly formed 101st Airborne Division learned to capture and defend roads, hills, bridgeheads, and airfields.

★★★★★★★★★★★★★

September 24, 1942
Dear Opal,

I arrived safe in Fort Bragg after an awful trip. The train was dirty and smoky. It was so crowded that I couldn't get to a washroom. When I got here, I was filthy. Haven't been in Fayetteville long enough to know anything about it. Miss you. Will write soon.

Love always,
Nicky

September 26, 1942
Dear Opal,

Darling, something is bothering me. I probably won't be able to send for you for three weeks, so don't stay in every night. Go out and have a good time. I trust you, and I know you will always be true.

I wrote my mother and told her that you and I are getting married. I hope she gives her blessing.

Last night I dreamed about you. We were married in the Church on a glorious spring day. You were dressed in white silk, and you wore a veil over your lovely face. I slipped a ring onto your finger, and the priest pronounced us man and wife. I lifted the veil and kissed you softly and sweetly. Then we melted into each other's arms.

We ran down the steps of the church, got into a car, and we drove to the country. We stopped at a little cottage with a rose-covered fence around the yard. I opened the gate, and I carried you up the path and across the threshold. We kissed again, and I vowed that I would always be true, and I would never leave you. Then, I woke up. You will be a darling little wife.

I Love You,
Nicky

September 27, 1942
Dear Opal,

I feel bad because I'm so far away from you. Today is dreary, but if you were here, my world would be bright and warm.

I found a jukebox in town with our number on it, and I played "I Think of You" twenty times. The waitress in the place thought I was crazy. I told her I was crazy in love. She asked, "With who?" and I said, "A girl in Alabama." She just laughed. If she thought I was kidding, she doesn't know what a beautiful Alabama girl you are.

Goodbye Hon,
Nicky

September 28, 1942
Dearest Opal,

We're taking it easy, but work will start soon, and I'll be glad. I'd rather work than sit around missing you. I put your picture in a frame. I will look at it every day, and when I go into battle, I will put it next to my heart.

Do you like that compact I sent? Every time you powder your nose, think of me.

Say, Honey Chile, remind Al [Romeo, son of the owners of the restaurant who worked with his parents, Opal, and Evelyn Ashwood at the restaurant.] that I won the baseball bet. I'll buy a few beers on him.

Lots and lots of love,
Nicky

September 28, 1942
Dear, Dear Nicky,

I am relieved to hear from you. I was afraid that anything might happen. I'm glad you weren't sent any farther than North Carolina. Will you be able to come to Birmingham? A weekend seems like a short time for such a long trip.

Love always,
Opal

September 29, 1942
Darling Opal,

Last night was awfully cold. I used two blankets and my overcoat to keep warm, but when I got out of bed, I almost froze to death. The food is good, and I'm eating most of it.

Yesterday twenty men from our outfit were sent across. They didn't have time to notify anyone. If I have to go, promise to wait for me, even though you might not get a letter for months. You said you would wait forever.

We had a blackout from 7:45 P.M. to 8:45 P.M. I lay in the dark thinking of you. I could see you in a beautiful green dress. You went to the phonograph and played one of our favorite songs. I turned the lights down low. Then you came to sit beside me. I took you in my arms and kissed you. I really enjoyed that blackout.

If you hurt me, I could never love again, but I know that you will never hurt me. I'll be thinking of you tonight at eight o'clock.

Last night I saw the movie "Desperate Journey" with Errol Flynn. It was very good. I wish you had been with me. This morning I was putting up curtains in my room in the barracks, and I thought, if Opal was here, she could certainly fix this room up.

I said that I want you to go out and have a good time. You said you don't care to go out with anyone but me. Baby, that's just what I wanted to hear.

I inquired about rooms downtown. They're hard to get, but I'll find a little paradise for you and me.

Someday I will have to go into battle. But I am fighting for people like us who want to marry and raise a family and live in freedom and peace. When the war is over, we will have a lifetime of love together.

I appreciate the kisses on your letters. I put my lips on the kisses and pretended I was kissing you. I could even taste the lipstick. Honey, send me at least one kiss with each letter.

Always Yours,
Nicky

September 30, 1942
Dearest Opal,

Today I'm the mail orderly. First thing this morning I went to the Post Office to get your sweet letter. You say it has been cold in Birmingham. It's cold here, too. Do you have an overcoat? You'll need one.

I have bad news. When I told my mother that we are getting married, she said she disapproves because we don't really know each other. I said that you mean everything to me, and I am going to marry you despite all h—. Hasn't she got some nerve? I am twenty-eight years old, and she is still trying to tell me what to do. I know you will be a fine wife.

Tonight I read this: "Those who love deeply never grow old. They may die of old age, but they die young."

Yours,
Nicky Boy

October 1942

As American aircraft bombed the Solomon Islands in the Pacific, a convoy of ships for Operation Torch, the invasion of North Africa, assembled in the Firth of Clyde on the east coast of Scotland. The convoy sailed for the Mediterranean, taking General George S. Patton's troops into action.

On the eastern front, the battle for Stalingrad raged.

In the battle of El Alamein in North Africa, British General Bernard Law Montgomery fought German General Erwin Rommel, the Desert Fox. Hitler ordered Rommel to resist to the last man:

> "Throw into the battle every man and every weapon still available . . . . Despite their superiority, the enemy too are at the limit of their resources. It would not be the first time in history that the stronger will triumphed over the stronger enemy battalions. You can show your troops no other road than that which leads to victory or to death." [4]

★ ★ ★ ★ ★ ★ ★ ★ ★ ★ ★ ★

October 2, 1942
Dearest Opal

I'm on guard duty for twenty-four hours. I'm commander of the guard, and I have nothing to do but think of you. I have your picture right here. My roommate says he's going to tell you a lot of lies about me, and maybe then, he can be your boyfriend. I told him that we are very much in love. He said I was a fool to trust any woman. I got mad and told him I wouldn't have your picture on my table if I didn't trust you.

Tell Al not to bet on the Yankees; the Cards are too good.

Loads and loads of love,
Nicky

October 3, 1942
Dear Darling Opal,

I know a gorgeous girl in Birmingham. She has red hair, green eyes, a cute turned-up nose, and a dazzling smile. She wears her clothes like a Fifth Avenue model. She is also hot-tempered. I fell for her the first time I saw her. About a month after I met her, I asked her to marry me. She said, "No," because she wasn't in love with me. Now, she loves me as I love her, and we'll be married soon. Her name is Opal. If you see her, tell her I said, "Hello."

Love,
Nicky

October 3, 1942
Nicky Darling,

Here I am at Romeo's and business is slow. It is time to play "I Think of You." Another song that expresses my feelings for you is "My Devotion" by Tommy Dorsey. I want to see you so much that I think you may come in at any minute. When the phone rings, I think you may be calling. Maybe I'll dream of you tonight. I pray that life will always bring the best for us.

Georgette [one of the women who lived in Opal's apartment house] didn't get the mail today, so I checked on the way to work, and I got your sweet letters. I read them walking down the street. The sun was shining bright, leaves were falling, and I spent a few golden minutes with you. I was thirty minutes late to work, but I didn't care. At last, I've found someone to whom I can give all the love in my heart. I want always to feel as I do now.

Lama [Lama Ganous was another friend who lived in the apartment house] and I visited her boyfriend Eddie who is in the hospital. He kissed me when I left, so I thought I should tell you.

I don't know if I'll be able to join you as soon as you'd like. I have some debts to pay, mostly doctor bills for treatment of my sinus problems. Don't offer to help. I'm used to taking care of myself.

Darling, I always wear my little wings and the cross you gave me, and I use my compact every day. Remember how I kissed you when you gave me the little wings?

Honey, don't write anything to hurt your mother. Make her understand that I love you, and I'll do all I can to be a good wife and daughter-in-law. Tell her I come from a good family. We don't have much money, but we have a good name, and we take pride in being good people.

Take care of yourself. If it's cold, wear heavy clothes and keep well for me. I'm glad you have healthy food. Eat as much as you can to give you strength for the work you have to do.

When we get married, who is going to be the head of the family? I think you should be.

Always yours,

Opal

October 3, 1942

Hello Darling,

I went downtown this afternoon, and every time I saw a soldier, I wished I would see you. I almost make myself believe that you could be here.

I picked up my pictures. I was thinking of you when the photographer snapped the shutter. My smile was a special smile for the boy I love.

After work, Lama and her friend Eddie and I walked to the Toddle House. We ate pie and drank coffee, and now I'm home and writing to you.

I love you,

Opal

October 4, 1942

Dearest Opal,

The night we played golf, you reminded me of a schoolgirl on her first date. You were very nervous. You didn't understand my teasing. But you were really cute . . . . Have you heard the song, "Be Careful with My Heart"? Well, you have my heart, so please don't break it.

Remember those two days I was absent [without leave]? The Captain fined me $50 a month for three months. But I don't care. The time I spent with you means more to me than a million dollars.

Lots of love,

Nicky

October 4, 1942

My Dearest Nicky,

Are you disappointed that I won't be able to come to Fayetteville right away? As I said, I have some debts to pay, so I want to continue to work . . . .

Darling, you mentioned getting an apartment for us. I don't care where we live. If we are together, one room will be heaven on earth.

Always yours,

Opal

October 4, 1942

Dearest Opal,

Your letter came at just the right time. I've been nervous and depressed all day. One of my men had an awful accident this morning. During bayonet practice, he was hit in the right eye. He lost one eye, and he may lose the other. A braver boy

I have never seen. He took it like a man. I was in the hospital from 9:30 A.M. To 6:00 P.M., and I must have smoked three packs of cigarettes.

All I know is that I love you. That you love me is a miracle. Without you, my world would be empty.

Love always,
Nicky

October 6, 1942
Dearest Darling Opal,

How's my little rebel—the gal from the land of the cotton pickers?

Sweetheart, I called my mother today, and she has only one thing on her mind—convincing me not to marry you. I told her how much we love each other, but she wanted to know if I had met your family. I lied and said that I had. I said that your family is Number One on the Hit Parade. I told her I have known you eight months, an exaggeration, but I know I love you, and that is all I need to know.

My mother said I always go against her. She said that if I married you, she would disown me. I choose you. You will always be my strength and guidance. I will fight well so I can come home to you.

I will love you until Doomsday.
Nicky

October 7, 1942
Dear Opal,

I haven't been able to eat for a few days. My soldier lost sight in both eyes . . . .

I enjoy reading your letters more than you know. I save them, and every so often, I take them out and read them over and over again.

Say Hon, have you ever cared for another boy as you care for me? When we are married, I want you to be sure; I don't want you to be sorry later on. If you discover you don't love me, you can be sorry for me, because . . .

I will always love you.
Nicky

[In 2003, Renaldo Angelini, a veteran who served in B Company, reported that the soldier regained sight in one eye.]

October 7, 1942
Dearest Nicky,

Mrs. Whitten *[the landlady at Opal's apartment house]* called me at work and said I had a letter from you. Al walked up the hill to get it for me. Wasn't that sweet? As soon as I got your letter, I played "Be Careful, It's My Heart" on the jukebox. The restaurant was empty, so Evelyn and I danced together. We felt foolish, but we waltzed and did the fox trot. She led.

It's "Fair Week" here in Alabama, and Ringling Brothers, Barnum, and Bailey are putting on the show. People who work at the fair and fair goers were in town, so we were busy.

I had a picture made for you. I was wearing my little wings. They show up well on the dress.

I love the cute little soldier boy *[a doll-like figure]* you gave me. He looks like you. I put him on my vanity next to your picture. Sometimes I talk to him. The other night as I was styling my hair, I said, "How do you like this style, Hon? And he said, "No, I don't like that; it looks prettier the other way." So I changed it back to the way it was. Think I'm crazy?

Opal's "cute little soldier boy."
Photo by Joe Loehle

I wonder how we'll get along when we're together every day and every night. I'm sure we'll be a loving couple. We like the same things—rain, snow, sports, movies, nice clothes, and a neat appearance.

Yours always,
Opal

October 8, 1942
My Darling Nicky Boy,

I have never been in love before. I think about you so much that sometimes I don't know what I am doing.

Don't worry about me walking home from work; Al usually walks with me. Sometimes Ms. Whitten, Lama and Eddie, and other friends keep me company. Al and Evelyn have been going together. Evelyn is crazy about Al, but. he was dating another girl. They quarreled and stopped seeing each other.

Honey, I didn't know Jim Johnson's girl very well. She worked at Romeo's, but I never went out with her. Mrs. Romeo got rid of her after only a few weeks. I don't like to talk about anyone, but Jim is playing with fire. She was a wild girl. She has been married twice, and she has a kid.

Darling, I'm not taking your mother's side, but I'm sure she loves you. She thinks she knows what's best for you. She had plans for you. It will take her a while to give them up.

I haven't told the family about us, but Pearl, the sister you met, told them. Then I talked to Mom [Louise Keith]. She said I must do what I think is best. I am the

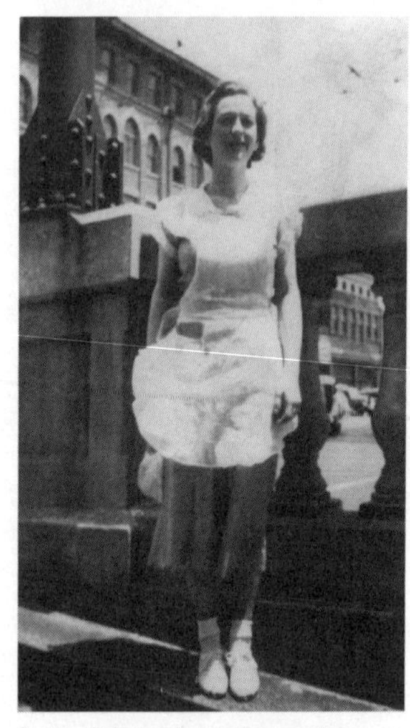

Evelyn Ashwood standing on the south end of the Rainbow Viaduct onTwentieth Street in Birmingham, 1942.

only one who knows what I want. She said she hopes I marry someone who will love me and make me happy.

Mom's life has been hard. Her mother died when she was twelve years old, and she raised her brothers and sisters. Mom's baby Clyde died of pneumonia when he was only a year old. Mom's oldest son, my brother Claude, was killed when he was only twenty-five years old. Mom had cancer, but she seems to be well. She never complains. She really loves her family and she would do anything for any of them. She worries about me living downtown. She wants me to live with her and Dad, but their place is too far out in the country. If I am going to work, I want to live in the city.

Darling, I don't need an engagement ring. I have my wings. And you probably can't afford to buy a ring now that you're paying that fifty-dollar fine for getting back to camp late. The plainest wedding band is all I want.

I'll love you always,
Opal

October 8, 1942
Dear Opal,

I wish I could take you to the Alabama State Fair. We'd watch the stock car races. I'd buy you a corn dog and cotton candy. I'd win the biggest prize in the shooting gallery, and we'd go through the Tunnel of Love.

If you wrote a hundred letters a day, I would stay up all night reading them. I wish I could write more. I get up at 5:30 A.M., go to breakfast, clean up the barracks, start work at 7:00 A.M., and work until 8:00 or 9:00 P.M. But I'm never too tired to write to you.

I got your gorgeous picture today, and I showed it to Butch [the English Bulldog Nicky mentioned in his first letter to Opal]. I asked him, "How do you like your mistress," and he wagged his tail, tilted his head back and forth, and barked. He loves you too.

Darling, you asked me if I have faith in God and in the power of prayer. I never was much of a believer, but now I know that God gave you to me to make me a better man. He will take good care of you while I'm gone. I say a prayer for you every night.

All my love,
Nicky

[Undated; probably written in mid-October]
Nicky Boy,

How are you doing? How's Fayetteville? We miss you. Nicky, you sure know your baseball. The Cards are killer dillers. Have you been listening to the Series? The Yanks have blown their tops. Come back to Birmingham soon, and we'll go to a few ball games. I'm enclosing money for you to celebrate the Cards win.

Your pal,
Al

October 11, 1942
Opal Honey,

Our love is sacred. I would never talk about our private moments, but some men brag about their conquests. Jim Johnson is up here, and he says bad things about the girl he dated in Birmingham—things I won't repeat. I think she is not the kind of girl you want for a friend. Don't say anything. I wouldn't want to hurt her feelings.

Friday night, we went on alert, and we were out until about 2:00 A.M. When I came in, I checked the mail first thing. I got four letters. And Darling, thank you for the cigarette case. I put your picture in it, so when I smoke, I can look at your charming smile.

Sgt. Franks said he would like to have his wife come from Fort Benning to Fayetteville, but he worries that she will be lonely if she doesn't know anyone. We talked about getting an apartment together so you girls could be company for each other. In Fayetteville a decent woman can't go anywhere without being bothered by a bunch of drunk soldiers. We could stay home and have our own party.

Until I had that row with my mother, she sent me a little money every month. I will not take any more money from her. My salary is $128 a month or about 30 dollars a week. Bus rides into town will be twenty cents a day; I'll eat in camp during the week and eat at home with you only on weekends. Do you think we can manage on that?

Now, don't get me wrong. I'm not broke. I bought a wedding present for you. I love you so much that I would quit drinking if you asked me to, and you know I like to have a drink or two.

Love always,
Nicky

October 12, 1942
Nicky Darling,

It's been a week since I received a letter. We were busy at work, and the jukebox was tripped. It played song after song with no one putting money in, and this is astonishing. About five minutes before 8 o'clock, P.M. "I Think of You" played. I asked Al and Evelyn if they had played that number, and they said they hadn't.

The Romeos hired a new girl, so I have the whole day off. I wish you were here. We've never had an entire day together.

Love always,

Opal

October 12, 1942

Dearest Opal,

When I come down, I want to meet your family. If they are like you, I'll love them.

I know it's a childish thing to do, but I kiss your pictures. I close my eyes, and I can feel your lips, your arms around me, and your soft body close to mine.

I received a telegram from my mother. She said, "Have you changed your mind?" I wrote to her, "I have not." If she will not recognize you as her daughter, I refuse to call her my mother.

Now, all I have is you. If you ever stopped loving me, it would be like a knife in my heart. It has been three weeks since I've seen you, and I worry that someday I will go away, and I may not come back for a very long time.

We got 150 new men today, and I'll be training them. I told them they might not know how to fight, but when I am through with them, they will be the best soldiers in the world. I said, "Six months ago, all I wanted was adventure, fun, women, and rum. Now I just want to win this war and get back to the girl I am going to marry." I asked them, "Do you want to return to your friends, sweethearts, and mothers?" They said, "Yes." I told them we will do the job right so we can all come home.

Are you proud of your future husband? Being one of the best soldiers in the army is something to be proud of. Unless we are starved to death. We have new rations, and they are bad.

Tomorrow, more soldiers from my outfit will leave for parts unknown. Next time, I may have to go. But Darling, keep your chin up. I wish we had met years ago. We could be happily married today and maybe have a couple of bambinos.

Always yours,

Nicky

October 16, 1942

Dear Opal,

I told you that my salary is $128 a month, but I forgot an extra $7 that I get, and after we are married, I'll get another $22. That comes to $157. Do you think we can live on $39 dollars a week? I'll give you all my pay, and you can spend it as you see fit . . . .

The news about Evelyn and Al is surprising. Does Mrs. Romeo approve?

Forever yours,

Nicky

Louise Leatherwood Keith, Pearl Keith and John Richard Keith, ca. 1912

October 16, 1942
Nicky Darling,

Please excuse the small notepaper. I don't want Mr. Romeo to see me writing. He gets mad, even if we are not busy. I told him to quit worrying. I'll stop all the letter writing soon. He said, "I shore will be glad." And people say southerners talk funny. I'm playing "I Think of You," "White Christmas," and "Indian Love Song" on the jukebox.

I want you to meet my family. Mom is fifty-nine, and she is a nice looking woman for her age; Dad is sixty-two, tall and slim; Pearl, the one you met, is my older sister. Dot is two years younger. She is a redhead, and she is married to a soldier. They have a baby, Patricia, who is two months old. James is eighteen; he's a little Irish hellcat. Freddie, the baby of the family, is fifteen. They are both big boys, bigger than I am. They work in town, but they live with Mom and Dad in the country. When you come down, we'll visit them, and we'll have one of the best southern-style dinners you ever ate.

Always yours,
Opal

October 17, 1942
Hello Opal Sweetheart,

We jumped today, and as we were flying to the drop zone, I wondered how long it would take you to get here if I got hurt. I would certainly want you near me.

Thanks for the stamps. The post office is about four miles away, but I'd travel a long road to get a stamp to send a letter to you.

When you come to Fayetteville, I'll be home with you every night unless I'm on guard duty or in the field.

Here is a picture of my dog Butch. Would you want him around the house to take care of you while I'm at camp? Or is he too big and ugly? He is an English bulldog. Some of the boys say he looks a lot like Winston Churchill.

I love you very, very much.
Nicky

October 18, 1942
Hello Opal Darling,

How is everything today? Full of happiness and joy? I got up this morning, went to church, and said a prayer for you. The whole world is beaming.

My mother is coming Wednesday. I'll go downtown and make hotel reservations for her. I know she is going to try to persuade me not to marry you. Don't worry. Nothing can change my decision.

My mother asked for your address, but I didn't give it to her. I was afraid she might write something that would hurt you.

Meeting your family is going to be fun. Does your dad drink? If so, I'll bring him some good whiskey. Tell me what he likes.

Your Yankee Soldier,
Nicky

October 19, 1942
Nicky, Darling,

I was supposed to be off today, but Mrs. Romeo called and said the new girl, Carol, is sick, so I had to work. We were busy. Alabama and Tennessee played today. Alabama won, naturally. But I'm not in the mood to celebrate. Half the time, when I'm supposed to be off, I'm called in to work. It makes me lose my Irish temper. . .

I love you. Here are three kisses for you. XXX
Love always,
Opal

WESTERN UNION
BMA 5198 BIRMINGHAM ALA 600 P M

SGT NICK BONILLA
CO B 502 PARACHUTE INFANTRY
101ST AIRBORNE DIVISION
FT BRAGG NCAR=

SOMEONE THINKING OF YOU TONIGHT.

LOTS OF LOVE,
OPAL

October 19, 1942
Darling Opal,

About 3:00 A.M., somebody came into my room, woke me up, and gave me a telegram. At first, I was mad, but then I laughed. Hon, you are so sweet to send me a telegram. Did you send it because you didn't write Saturday and Sunday?

I listened to the Alabama/Tennessee game. Alabama beat Tennessee 8 to 0. When I come home, I'll take you to an Alabama game. I'll buy you one of those chrysanthemums that the girls wear. We'll sit in the stands, eat roasted peanuts, and drink Coca-Cola.

What do we need to do to get married? Do we need medical tests? Where do we get a license? Who will perform the ceremony? I want to know exactly what we're going to do when I get down there.

Jim Johnson went to Pennsylvania to marry his girl. I asked him about the girl in Birmingham, and he told me that she did not mean a thing to him; she was just another playmate. But let's keep that to ourselves.

Only two days before my mother arrives in Fayetteville; then we will have a second front, right here in North Carolina.

Goodnight Mrs. Bonilla,
Nicky

October 20, 1942
Nicky Darling,

Did you get the telegram? I told the clerk to get it to you before 8:00 P.M. I've never written so many letters in my life. I usually don't like to write, but now I enjoy it.

You asked me if I thought I could manage on $39 a week. I hate to think I would have to manage anyone's money. I'm a spendthrift. I buy too many dresses, hats, handbags, and shoes. Don't you think I should continue to work after we are married? I've been working for seven years. I don't know what I'd do with a lot of free time.

I almost had a fit this afternoon. I wore my wings home last night, and then I couldn't find them. I looked all over the restaurant, and I searched my apartment. I finally found them. They were on my yellow sweater. I wore it with the buttons down the back, and I pinned the wings on the front, (really the back). When I found them, I said, "Oh, Thank God."

I'll love you forever,

Opal

October 20, 1942

Dear Opal,

I didn't get a letter from you. I did receive two short notes. Darling, please write a long letter. I want to hear all about you and your family and friends. I've written you every day for the last eight days. I want you to write to me every day. Those little notes make me think you're getting lazy or bored.

As I said before, if you find someone else you care for, just let me know. I won't stand in your way, but . . .

I'll love you forever,

Nicky

October 20, 1942

Darling Opal,

Honey, I've been pestering the company commander to give me a pass, but he refuses. If he refuses much longer, I'm going to take a few days leave on my own hook [without official permission].

Sometimes I get mad, not at anybody in particular, but mad that I'm so far away from you. Soon we'll be together every night

Even in the field, I think of you every night at 8:00 P.M. Since we've been dating, you've missed writing me only fifteen days—when I left Ft. Benning, when I went to New York, when I went to Ft. Bragg. Your letters mean everything to me.

Will you be ready to come to Fayetteville after we are married? I want you with me so much. We can go bowling, dancing, and to football games. We can walk on sunny days and moonlit nights. We'll have a swell time.

Don't work too hard; save all your strength for me, because when we're married, you're going to need it.

Should I buy your wedding ring, or shall we pick it out together?

Your future husband,

Nicky

October 20, 1942
Nicky Dearest,

Tonight Mr. Romeo said, "I don't think that boy is Italian. He's a Jew if there ever was one." *[Nicky's mother was a second- or third-generation Italian, and his father was of Colombian descent. The family lived in Puerto Rico until Nicky was six years old. Nicky did not speak Italian.]* I told him that I didn't care if you were an Arab. A person's nationality is not important, only his character.

I'm sorry your mother doesn't want me as a daughter-in-law, but I will always treat her as well as I would want her to treat me. Please don't quarrel with your mother. She deserves your respect. I wish she was like my mother. Mom says that we have a right to make our own decision.

Darling, I'm sitting in the back booth where we sat the last time we were together. We snuggled in the corner so no one could see us kissing goodnight. I hated to see you leave.

Remember when you invited me to your hotel room for a drink, and then you said I had done a dangerous thing. You said I don't know men, that another man could have taken advantage of me. You were right. I don't know men. I had never been in a hotel room in my life. I was hurt that you would test me—that you would ask me to do something and then disapprove of me for doing it. I wish that had never happened. But no matter what,

I'll love you always,
Opal

October 21, 1942
Dear Opal,

Honey, we'll have to talk about you working after we get married. You can't work in a restaurant in an army town. What those girls have to put up with from soldiers is pitiful . . . .

Tonight I tried to call you, but I couldn't make the connection.

Love,
Nicky

October 22, 1942
Darling Opal,

I just got back from town. I was with my mother most of the day. She arrived about 8:00 A.M. She looked tired, so I took her to the hotel, and she slept until 1:00 P.M. We ate lunch, and then went back to the hotel. That's when the war started. My mother asked me all about you—your age, your education, your religion, your family. I answered her questions as politely as I could. Then she said you weren't good enough for me. I blew up! I told her that I love you and I am going to marry you despite all hell.

She began to cry. She said I always defy her—I refused to take piano lessons; I refused to go to college; refused to marry the girl she picked out for me. She said I am ungrateful. I don't appreciate the sacrifices she has made for me.

Then I saw something I had never seen before. My mother is a good actress. Fire came to her eyes, and she said if I married you, I could never call her "Mother" again. I stormed out and went to the nearest bar for a good stiff drink. Don't worry, Honey. Just love me and everything will be all right.

Your future spouse,
Nicky

October 24, 1942
Hi Opal, Sweet.

I tried to call you at the restaurant, but I couldn't make the connection.

I wish you could have a shower, a church wedding, and a party that all your family could attend, but in this crazy world, we don't have time. I want us to marry as soon as we can so we can spend every minute together.

Do I miss you? Would the Smith Brothers miss their beards? Would Joe DiMaggio miss his favorite bat? Would Fred Astaire miss his dancing shoes? Would Bing Crosby miss crooning?

I'm glad you like those magazine pictures. The 503rd has some good-looking soldiers, but we in the 502nd are better trained, and we are better fighters.

Always,
Nicky

October 25, 1942
Nicky, Darling,

Why haven't I heard from you? I haven't received a letter in eight days. Bad thoughts stick in my mind like needles and pins. I want a good long letter telling me what you're doing and why you haven't written.

Little Michael Romeo, Frank's son, still remembers you. I asked him, "Where's Nicky Boy?" He said, "Nicky Boy gone; gone bye-bye."

Jim Johnson's girl came into the restaurant last night. She was with a middle-aged fellow, and she was quite reserved. When I got her alone, I asked why she wasn't wearing Jim's wings. She said she gave them back. She said that when Jim left, she met this new fellow, and she is crazy about him.

When I left the restaurant, it was raining. I waited and waited for a cab, but not a one came by. So I decided to run home. The rain was fresh and cool, and although I got wet, I didn't mind. I was wearing a hat with a high brim, and when I got to the apartment house, it was full of water, like a bucket. I took my hat off and threw the water into the yard. Then, I laughed. I was happy—happy because I am in love.

I get off early tonight, and I'm going home—alone.

Love always,
Opal

October 25, 1942
Opal Dearest,
Isn't "White Christmas" a beautiful song? Remember, we were together the first time we heard it. I am looking forward to spending Christmas with my wife.

You say you haven't made plans for our marriage. Darling, Uncle Sam is my boss, and I'm on his time schedule. Whatever we do, we'll have to do quick. Every hour and every day that we are together will be precious. Al can be my best man, and Evelyn can be your bridesmaid.

Yours,
Nicky

October 26, 1942
Darling Nicky,
This morning, Lama went out to get the mail, and when she came back, she said, "Nothing from Nicky Boy." I was so disappointed I almost cried. She laughed, threw two letters and a package in my lap, and left me alone to read my mail.

I was afraid you might not be able to write while your mother was there. I thought she might get our letters and destroy them.

I received the pictures from *Look*. I am very proud of my fiancé, "one of Uncle Sam's most versatile fighting men," a paratrooper. I wish the pictures showed the 502nd instead of the 503rd.

Darling, I don't want a shower or wedding party. I've been away from home so long that I've lost touch with my school friends. I don't go to church, so I don't know many people. And these days, you can't tell who is a friend and who isn't. Let's have a private wedding celebration.

Love always,
Opal

October 26, 1942
Darling Nicky,
Once you asked me if I wanted someone fighting the war for me. I never thought about that, but now, I'm betting everything on you. I know you're a good soldier and a good man. You'll be a fine husband. You'll have to be the boss. I'm not tough enough. I'll love taking orders from you. We'll just think of the army as a regular job. It's an important and a dangerous job, but we'll make the best of it. [Paratroopers were a first-strike force, and for each one in combat, nine non-combatants were required. Nicky's job was indeed dangerous.]

I bought some paper for airmail letters. The paper I had was too thick, and it made my letters bulky. Now I can write more pages.

I got a card from the photographer saying that my pictures were ready, so I sent the Postal Telegraph girl (they have girls now) to get it. Then I had to think how to mail the picture so it wouldn't get bent. Hope you get it in good shape.

"Hot news! Right off the press! Read all about the great love affair!" Evelyn and Al are dating. Al was dating a girl named Marie, but they broke up. Marie heard that Al was dating Evelyn, and Marie called Evelyn at the restaurant. Marie said that Al was in love with her and had asked her to marry him. Evelyn wanted to know why Al was dating her if he was so in love with Marie. Then Al talked to Marie. He said he thought a lot of her, and he had enjoyed dating her, but he had made her no promises. When Al hung up the phone, Evelyn fainted. I was frightened. I had never seen anyone faint.

We picked Evelyn up out of the floor and sat her on a chair. We put cold cloths on her head and slapped her wrists. Finally, she woke up. About that time, Marie walked in the door. She, Evelyn, and Al raised hell for about an hour.

Then Mrs. Romeo came out of the kitchen. She didn't know what was going on, but she tried to make Evelyn go into the kitchen. Evelyn wouldn't go. After a while, Marie left, and then Mrs. Romeo raised hell with Al and Evelyn.

Mrs. Romeo doesn't know that Al and Evelyn are dating; she doesn't want Al to date anyone. I'm glad your mother is in New York.

Tonight I'll say a prayer for our happiness.

Love always,

Opal

October 27, 1942

Hello Opal, Sweetheart,

Do you remember that I got 150 new men to train? I took them out to the rifle range, and about 20 of them are mighty poor shots. I may have to get rid of them. I'd hate to do it, but I don't want to fight with men who can't shoot. I want to come home safe and sound. Soldiers are fighting and dying every day so we can live free from the interference of a bunch of Nazis and backstabbing Japs . . . .

Goodnight Darling,

Nicky

October 27, 1942

Nicky Darling,

I received your letter today, and I was glad to get it even though you scolded me. I guess I deserved a scolding for not writing often enough or long enough. Last night I wrote a letter so long that you'll get tired reading it. You'll yawn, rub your eyes, and fall asleep.

I just heard Dick Jergens on the radio playing "Every Night about This Time." I love to listen to our favorite songs and think of you. I'm fond of music, but I can't sing or play an instrument.

I'm counting the days until I see you.

Opal

October 27, 1942
Nicky, Sweetheart,

Everyone has noticed a change in me. Customers say, "Your eyes are sparkling. You must be in love." I say, "I'm very much in love." I've always heard that love is sweet misery, and now I believe it. I'm sad. I'm happy. I'm worried. I'm excited. I'm in a daze.

I usually get up at about 8:00 A.M. I sit at a little table in my apartment and look out the window watching for the postman. I drink a cup of coffee and I think of you. When I see the postman coming up the walk, I scram down the hall as fast as lightning.

The postman laughs at me. Sometimes he says, "Nothing today," and he sees that I am disappointed. Sometimes he says, "If I want to see you smile, I'd better give you your letters."

If the mail doesn't come until after I've gone to work, I pay someone from Postal Telegraph thirty-five cents to go to the house to get my mail and deliver it to me at the restaurant. I'd gladly pay any amount for a letter from you.

Loving you always,
Opal

October 29, 1942
Dearest Opal,

You go to my head like fine champagne. Every time I hear a sweet song, I think of you. Every night I want to dream of you.

I received your pictures, and I put them in frames. The Captain came into my room and saw your picture. He asked, "Who is the pretty girl?" I said, "That's the girl I'm going to marry. He said, "When are you going to get married?" and I said, "First chance I get." He said I could have six days off starting Nov 9. That means I can leave Nov 6 and be there Saturday night November 7. Isn't that swell?

I'm sorry to hear about Al's love troubles. It's not very sporting of his old girl friend to try to hold on to Al. If he loves someone else, she should step aside. What would you do? Would you fight for your man?

When I see you, I'm going to take you in my arms and kiss you and kiss you. Remember how I unscrewed the light bulb in the hallway at your apartment house and kissed you in the dark? I never wanted to say goodnight.

Forever yours,
Nicky

October 30, 1942
Dear Sweetheart,

I feel terrible about quarrelling with my mother, but how would I feel if I gave you up to please her? If I lost you, I would ask to be sent across the Pacific right away. I tried to call you at the restaurant, but I missed you. We're going to the field for a few days, and I won't be able to write, but when I get back, I'll write a good long letter.

Your future husband,
Nicky

October 30, 1942
Nicky Darling,

How are you Sweetheart? I am blue. I just got back from town and Evelyn told me you called. I'm so d— mad. I want to talk to you so much, and then when I step out, you call. I'm so upset that I probably won't be able to work the rest of the day. My stomach is in a knot, and my hands are shaking.

You asked me about the letters mailed from Anniston and Montgomery. Georgette was going to mail them for me downtown, but she forgot both times, and she mailed one from Anniston where she was visiting her boyfriend and one from Montgomery where she was visiting her mother. Guess you thought I was really traveling, but I don't want to go anywhere unless you are there . . . .

Always yours,
Opal

October 31, 1942
Dearest Opal,

I'm sure you know that I tried to call. It took me two hours to get that call through and then I didn't get to talk to you. I heard the Alabama/Georgia game on the radio today. I bet on Alabama, and the team did me dirt by losing. But Alabama is still a great state. That's where my girl lives.

Have to go. The Captain wants to talk to me about the new men.

Loads of love,
Nicky

[Nicky was Sergeant of First Squad, Second Platoon, B Company. Men in the squad were, Corp. J.W. Alsgiver, Pvt. E. L. Hetrick, Pvt. W. W. Leonard, Pvt. B. Myers, Pvt. H. T. O' Hagan, Pvt. C. Pentz, Pvt. M. Logorda, Pvt. H.W. Butcher, Pvt. W. S. Caraway, Pvt. A. P. (Pete) Botzis, and Pvt. T.W. Farricker.]

Georgette Seals joined the Womens Marine Corps in 1943.

November 1942

As Nicky and Opal planned to marry, Japanese troops hammered American soldiers and sailors in the Pacific. German troops threatened the Balkans, and Wolf Packs, German submarines, prowled British shipping lanes.

Opening a new front in Europe or Africa would engage Axis troops while Allies prepared for a cross-channel invasion of Germany from England. As British troops commanded by General Montgomery fought Field Marshal Rommel's forces in the east, American soldiers would attack from the west. General Dwight D. Eisenhower held a secret meeting with General Henri Giraud on November 7. Giraud, the hero of the battle of Verdun in World War I, had led the French army against German invaders in 1940, but French forces were defeated, and Giraud was imprisoned. He escaped and fled to Algiers. General Eisenhower persuaded General Giraud to take command of French forces in Algeria, Morocco, and Tunisia after the coming invasion, Operation Torch.

On November 7, men of the 509th Parachute Infantry Regiment flew 1,600 miles from England to Oran, Algeria, for the first combat jump by American paratroopers. Led by Col. Edson Raff, the 509th teamed up with British and French troops to seize airfields and ports between Casablanca and Algiers. Axis forces could not use these ports as submarine bases or areas of operation. The Axis launched counterattacks with fighters, bombers, and ground troops brought in by air transport.

Allied paratroopers fought in Tunisia until December 1, when they were relieved by infantry. The first African-American female nurses to serve overseas were sent to North Africa.

Operation Torch demonstrated to Allied commanders that paratroopers were effective quick-strike forces, but once on the ground, they could be surrounded and outgunned. They could not operate over large areas without logistical support, motor transportation, artillery, and anti-tank weapons. The United States military drafted more men and plants worked at capacity to meet the demand for war materiel.

★ ★ ★ ★ ★ ★ ★ ★ ★ ★ ★ ★ ★ ★

November 2, 1942
Dear Nicky,

My brother James came to see me. He is going into the Army Air Corps. I hate to see him leave. I think military service will be a good thing for him, but he is so young. [James was eligible for the draft, and he was "so mad [he] couldn't see straight" about the Japanese attack on Pearl Harbor, so he volunteered.]

I'm sitting here in the middle of my bed surrounded by your letters and pictures. If you could see me now, you'd think I'm ugly. I'm wearing a gown and a housecoat, and I'm barefoot. My hair is in my face, and I'm wearing no make-up.

James Keith wears his Army Air Corps uniform.

I look like a witch. Of course, you will never see me looking like I look now.

I wear my little silver wings all the time, and people ask, "Do you have a boyfriend who's a paratrooper?" Then I have the great pleasure of telling them all about you. A good many soldiers come into Romeo's, but when they see my wings, they don't even bother asking for dates. They say, "Oh, look. She's wearing silver wings for someone."

Mrs. Romeo tries to talk me out of getting married. She says that all men are S.O.B.s. But she doesn't know my Nicky Boy. Do you want me to be a Catholic? I will be, if you want. I know my family would object, but that doesn't matter. I believe we can overcome all obstacles and make our love last a lifetime.

Love always,
Opal

November 3, 1942
Nicky Darling,

Today I told Mrs. Romeo I was going to quit, and she threw a fit. She said I should have given her two weeks notice. She is mad. Do you think she would give me two weeks notice if she was going to fire me?

Several women, including Mrs. Romeo, have told me that marriage is no bed of roses, and I am very nervous. I know if you were here, I'd feel calm and sure of myself.

A friend drove me to the country to visit Mom and Dad. I told them about you. They are happy I've found someone I love. Mom said she is sorry that we'll marry so quick, but in wartime, we must make sacrifices. Mom said you could stay with the family for a few days, but she would be ashamed of the place where they live. She and Dad used to have a nice house, but they have lost everything, and are just trying to get by.

Are you a good sergeant for the new fellows? Do you try to talk tough and look mean? I'll bet they like you.

Love always,
Opal

November 3, 1942
Dearest Opal,

I'm sitting here in the service club listening to the jukebox. You should be proud of your brother going into the Air Corps. He'll learn how to take care of himself.

Darling, this will probably be the last letter I'll write before I leave Fayetteville. I am happy to be coming to Birmingham to marry the girl I love.

I did not know the meaning of the word "LOVE" until I met you. My feelings for you are tender and sweet. I am almost sorry that we met. When I have to leave you, I will feel like a dozen devils are driving pitchforks into my soul.

Always,
Your Nicky Boy

November 5, 1942
Dear Nicky,

I quit my job, and I played "I Think of You" on the jukebox for the last time. I'll miss Evelyn, Al, and Mr. and Mrs. Romeo. They are like family. I feel strange. I won't know what to do with myself if I'm not working. The girls here at the apartment house are talking about renting my little place to one of the girls who is sharing an apartment.

My brothers and my sisters gave me money to pay my doctor bills [for treatment of sinus problems]. I am proud of them for being so generous. They don't have much, and I'm grateful for their help. I bought two large metal trunks for shipping my things to North Carolina.

Oh Honey, I'm not sure I'll make a good wife. I don't know much about cooking or housekeeping. When I iron, I put more wrinkles in the clothes than I get out. But, I'll try my best.

Love always,
Opal

November 6, 1942
Darling Nicky,

I got the telegram. You are arriving Sunday morning at 5:30. Will I be there to meet you? You can bet your life. I'll be nervous as the devil. I probably won't sleep at all Saturday night.

Love always,
Opal

November 7, 1942
Dearest, Darling, Nicky

In about six hours, I'll see you. I feel like I've been waiting for you forever. I drank coffee with Lama; then I walked over to see my sister Pearl, and my nephew

Farris. I cleaned my apartment. Now I need to get some sleep so I can get up at 4:30 A.M. and be ready to meet you at 5:30 A.M. I love you.

Always yours,

Opal

Chapter Two

Sgt. and Mrs. Nicholas L. Bonilla

November 1942

Opal said she had never been in love before, and Nicky was not sure she loved him enough to marry him and be faithful. He knew that many soldiers who were engaged, even married men, got "Dear John" letters.

Nicky had little money to support a wife, but he knew that some women married soldiers just to get an allotment. He heard soldiers say in jest that G.I. meant "Got Insurance." Nicky could ship out any day. As a paratrooper, he would be among the first to fight. He would leave behind a woman who would become bored and lonely. He might be wounded or killed. If Nicky married Opal, he would defy his mother, take on responsibility for a wife, and act contrary to the teachings of the Catholic Church. Additionally, single men were believed to be better soldiers than married men. Henry A. Bowman, writing in *American Magazine* in August 1942 said, "These hasty marriages . . . impair the efficiency of our fighting men. Military authorities will tell you that a bachelor makes a much more determined and fearless fighter than a married man." [5]

Until she met Nicky, Opal had been determined not to marry. Opal was striking, but she did not see her own beauty. She was wary of the attention men gave her. She enjoyed dating, but she had never felt deep affection for anyone outside her family.

Opal knew that marriage was no guarantee of love or security. Her parents' marriage was trouble-filled. Her mother, Louise Keith had given birth to seven children; one died as an infant. Opal's father, John Keith lost a good job during the Depression and lost the family's savings in a bank failure. After that, he struggled to support his wife and children. He operated a coal mine, where his eldest son was killed in a cave-in. Louise blamed John for operating the mine unsafely. Opal's parents were often in conflict. Their marriage was not one Opal wanted to emulate.

Opal liked working and taking care of herself. She was devoted to her women friends. She worked six days a week; she said she was too lazy to go to church on Sunday, her only day off.

If Opal married Nicky and moved to Fayetteville, she would give up her independence, leave her family and friends, and take on the role of cook and housekeeper, a role for which she was not prepared.

Although Opal took Nicky to visit her sister Pearl, brother- in-law Emmett, and nephew Farris, she did not take him to the country to meet the rest of the family. Opal's ancestors fought in the American Revolution and the Civil War, and Opal was proud of her family, but she was ashamed of the place where they lived.

John Keith had sold the family home, bought a small coal mine in Jefferson County, and built rough shelters for men who worked for him. He moved his family into one of those. After having lived a middle-class life in a small town, Louise was now cooking on a wood stove and carrying water from a spring. Dorothy, Opal's younger sister, lived with her mother, father, and two brothers. Her husband was in the army, and Dot cared for her baby, Patricia, and helped her mother cook, wash, and clean for a family of six. Teenagers Fred and James worked in Birmingham and at home.

Opal feared that Nicky, who grew up in Manhattan, might think, as his mother did, that Opal and her family were not good enough for him.

Nicky expected to meet Opal's family, and as Opal delayed introducing them, Nicky's uncertainty grew. Nicky accused Opal of marrying him for an allotment and insurance, of being ashamed of him, of being anti-Catholic, of having a shameful family, and a shameful past.

Opal did not quarrel with Nicky. She said that she had told him the whole truth about herself and her family. No matter what he might say to her, she would always love him. She would prove it by marrying him. She had given him her heart, and now she surrendered her pride. Opal and Nicky were married November 10, 1942 by Reverend James Cantrell, Pastor of the Third Presbyterian Church at 617 South 22nd Street in Birmingham. Evelyn was Opal's Maid of Honor, and Al was Nicky's Best Man. The couple honeymooned at the Redmont Hotel. Because of their quarrel, Opal remained in Birmingham rather than going to Fayetteville as she had planned to do. Nicky returned to Fayetteville on November 14 or 15.

The Third Presbyterian Church in Birmingham

November 15, 1942
Darling Nicky,

I visited my sister Pearl today. Pearl likes you, and she says you will always be welcome to visit. Emmett, my brother-in-law, likes you, and I know you will like him. Emmett borrowed a car, and we drove to the country to visit Mom and Dad.

Mom gave me h—. She said I hurt you when I refused to bring you to meet the family. She was right. I told her that if she would forgive me, I'd never let false pride take hold of me again. Please forgive me. We would not have quarreled if I had taken you to meet my family.

But some of the things you said to me hurt. I've dated many boys, but I've never loved anyone but you. I can look God in the face and say I've lived a clean life. If you don't believe me, I'll just have to prove it by being the most loving, most faithful wife I can be.

Always yours,
Opal

November 18, 1942
My Dearest Nicky,

I miss my husband. We have been married one week and one day. Darling, I was thrilled to get the first letter addressed to Mrs. Nicholas Bonilla; I love you more than life itself, and I hope you will always love me.

I am trying to learn all I need to know to be a good wife. I want to plan delicious meals and cook all your favorite foods. I'm going to knit socks for you. I'll buy heavyweight wool yarn. What size do you wear? [Opal did not know how to knit, and despite her offer to make socks, she never learned to knit.]

I want to manage our money wisely. I'm helping Nancy, another girl who lives in the apartment house. She is deeply in debt. She owes three loan companies, and the interest she pays is outrageous. She gives me her pay, I pay her bills, and I give her an allowance.

I can't get used to spending money I didn't earn. It seems to go so fast. Maybe I should go back to work for a while. Finding a job here at Christmas time would be easy. Mrs. Romeo called me yesterday and asked me to come back to work at the restaurant. She needs me on the four o'clock to midnight shift. What do you think? I'll do what you want me to do.

Tonight I went to the Third Presbyterian Church where we were married. Rev. Cantrell said to tell you "Hello." He said he will write to you. I am going back to service on Sunday. I have our marriage certificate, and I'll send it to you.

You will always be my only love.
Opal

Company B. Nicky is seated eighth from the left.

November 19, 1942
Dear Opal,

How are you, Darling? I'm tired and numb from lack of sleep, and I am so lonely without you I can't stand it. Please come to Fayetteville as quick as you can. Send me a telegram so I can meet you at the station. And bring our marriage license.

Thank you for the stamps. Mrs. Bonilla is very kind to Sgt. Bonilla. You're knitting socks? I need size 11 1/2, and I think gray heavy weight will be just right. You'd like to use the name "Loren" because it is one of my family names? I don't want you to do that. I like the name "Opal." It is a beautiful name for an enchanting girl.

Tonight I'm writing from the guardhouse. The bugler is blowing taps, and it sounds sweet and sad. Honey, don't expect too much. Fayetteville is just a soldier's town—full of greasy-spoon restaurants, rough bars, tattoo parlors, and souvenir shops. I hope you won't care what the town is like as long as we're together.

I found a room in a nice boarding house. But it is just empty space until you come. When you are here, it will be filled with happiness. Since I'll be staying in town with you, I'm sending Butch to New York. I will always love you, and I will try to be a good husband. I miss you 60 seconds every minute, 60 minutes every hour, and 24 hours every day.

Yours,
Nicky

November 20, 1942
Opal Darling,

When you come up here, you'll knock the eyes out of these hicks. You are stunning.

Do you need money for train fare or other travel expenses? If I don't have it, I'll borrow it. If I can't borrow it, I'll steal it. Go to Terminal Station and buy a ticket for Fayetteville, North Carolina. Try to get an afternoon train. You may have

to change trains, but you can ship your baggage straight through to Fayetteville. By the way, are you learning to cook?

I'll love you forever, and that's a long time.

Nicky

November 21, 1942

Hello Nicky Darling,

I'm so glad you want me to come to Fayetteville. Since I quit work, I have too much time on my hands. I want to be with you. I saw Dr. Fox today. He said, "Hello Mrs. Sergeant. How is Sarge?" I asked him to give me medicine to treat my sinus problems at home.

I stopped at Walgreen's to have my prescriptions filled, and I heard 'White Christmas." I thought how happy I'll be spending Christmas with you.

I've packed some things, and I'll take everything else to Pearl's. I'll try to be ready to leave by Saturday. If I can come before, will you meet me?

I love you; I love you; I love you.

Opal

November 27, 1942

Dear Mom,

Here I am in North Carolina with Nicky. I arrived Sunday night at midnight, and Nicky was right there at the station to meet me. The trip wasn't too bad. It took me more than twenty-six hours to get here. I changed trains three times, and every train was late. The depots were clouded with cinders, smoke, and dust. I have never been so soot covered.

Nicky rented a room for us at the hotel. He was off all day Monday, and we found some good places to eat. Monday night we saw the movie "Sunny," and after the show, Enoch Light and his band played. They are going from here to play at the Astor Hotel in New York.

I'm sorry I didn't see you before I left, but I decided to go as soon as I got Nicky's letter.

Nicky is working today, and I'm washing stockings and underwear. We are moving to a boarding house where we can live inexpensively.

Give my love to all,

Opal

★★★★★★★★★★★★★

Opal and Nicky lived on Gillespie Street in Fayetteville in the home of Mr. and Mrs. Jetton. The newlyweds enjoyed eating out, dancing, and going to movies. When the weather was warm, the couple sat on the porch of their Victorian boarding house and read the *New York Times*. Opal met some of the men of B Company including Renaldo Angelini, "Pete" Botzis, and "Sadie" Hawkins.

★★★★★★★★★★★★★

DECEMBER 1942

As Nicky and Opal celebrated their first Christmas together, American armed forces fought Japanese troops at Guadalcanal.

British Member of Parliament Sydney Silverman reported to the House of Commons that Nazis had murdered two million Jews.

Heavy fighting continued in Stalingrad. Royal Air Force (R.A.F.) planes based in Egypt hit Naples and Turin. In Tunisia, fourteen British and ten Axis planes were shot down. R.A.F. planes based in Britain struck Munich.

JANUARY 1943

The New Year found U. S. and Australian forces fighting Japanese troops in New Guinea.

Russian forces destroyed German armies at Stalingrad.

In the Casablanca conferences, Roosevelt, Churchill, and Stalin decided to open a second front in Europe. French General Giraud and General Charles de Gaulle became co-presidents of the French Committee of National Liberation. As Giraud had done, De Gaulle led a French army against the German invasion, but failed to stop it. When France fell, De Gaulle fled to England. He urged the French in colonies to continue to resist. He was recognized as the leader of the "Free French." Marshal Henri-Philippe Petain, age eighty-three, became head of the pro-German Vichy government.

Germany mobilized all men between the ages of sixteen and sixty-five, and all women between the ages of seventeen and forty-five for war work. The Luftwaffe, the German air force, raided London and other targets in the southeast of England in the first night attacks since May 1941.

The U.S. 8th Air Force flew missions over Germany, bombing warehouses and industrial plants. The R.A.F. made daylight raids on Berlin.

★★★★★★★★★★★★★

In Fayetteville, Nicky and Opal settled into a routine as a married couple. Nicky trained at Fort Bragg, and Opal worked in Rayless Department Store. The two were so nearly the same size and of such similar coloring that people often asked if they were brother and sister. Nicky was proud to tell everyone that the woman beside him was his wife.

Nicky loved Opal's voluptuous figure, but he did not want her to gain much weight. He teased her about her wide hips. He called her "Crisco," fat in the can. On January 9, 1943, Nicky and Opal started a fitness program. They measured their bodies. Each wrote measurements on an envelope. Nicky weighed 132 pounds. His ankles were nine inches in diameter; his calves fourteen inches, his thighs eighteen inches, his waist twenty-six inches, and his chest thirty-nine inches.

Opal did not record her weight. Her ankles were nine inches in diameter; her calves were fourteen inches, her thighs were eighteen inches, her hips forty inches, her waist twenty-nine inches, and her bust was thirty five inches.

Opal and Nicky planned to manage "their" weight by walking and avoiding sugar, bread, and fried foods.

When business at Rayless declined in January, Opal was let go. Nicky was "busted" on January 28. He had left the base without official permission. It was apparent that Opal would have to return to Birmingham.

February 1943

On February 8, U.S. troops captured Guadalcanal in the Pacific.

In the European Theater of Operation, R.A.F. bombers attacked Milan.

In Stalingrad, the Russians held against German attacks, and Nazi resistance ended. From Britain, the R.A.F. and American Army Air Corps began bombing Germany around the clock. British crews made night raids, and Americans flew daylight missions.

The U.S. War Manpower Commission and the Selective Service set a goal of inducting 12,000 men each day. All able-bodied men eighteen years old to thirty-eight years old were eligible for the draft. Their term of service would be from their induction to six months after the end of hostilities, or "for the duration." Previously, fathers and workers in essential industries were exempt. In one year, more men were drafted than had served in the entire American Army during World War I.

★★★★★★★★★★★★★

Because Nicky lost rank and pay and Opal was not working, the couple could not afford to pay for their room in the boarding house. With great reluctance, Opal returned to Birmingham in mid-February. Opal suspected that she might be pregnant, and she visited a physician who confirmed what she had suspected. Opal was worried about having a child to care for when Nicky's future was so unsettled. Nicky hoped to go to O.C.S. (Officer's Candidate School) so he could remain in the United States with his wife and child.

Since Opal had given up her apartment at Ms. Whitten's house, she lived with her sister Pearl, her brother-in-law Emmett, and her nephew Farris.

★ ★ ★ ★ ★ ★ ★ ★ ★ ★ ★ ★ ★

February 17, 1943
Nicky Darling,

I miss you more than ever. I arrived in Birmingham at 7:15 A.M. The trip was very tiring. I had an hour and a half layover in Florence, South Carolina, and then another forty-minute wait in Samson. We arrived in Augusta, Georgia, at 2:50 P.M. and missed the connecting train. The next train out didn't come until 2:00 A.M., so I took the bus at 4:15 P.M. I got to Atlanta at 10:25 P.M. and waited only until 12:55 A.M. for the train. The train was full. I wish you had been with me so I could have leaned on your shoulder to rest. Some soldiers lay in the aisles and slept on the floor.

Because I couldn't get up and walk around, my legs swelled enormously. I was embarrassed. When I got here, I took a taxi to Pearl's. We talked and I fell asleep about 11:00 A.M., so I'm well rested.

Hay Street, looking west, Fayetteville, North Carolina from a postcard, ca. 1941.

Emmett went to town and got my watch. I'm happy to have it. I love it because you gave it to me as my wedding present.

Farris wrote you a letter. He is quite smart for a six-year old.

Love always,

Opal

February 18, 1943

Nicky Darling,

This afternoon I got some Beville's Lotion for your feet. [Beville's Lotion was a treatment for "dough foot," a fungal infection soldiers contracted while wearing wet boots for several days or weeks.]

I returned the portion of the train ticket I didn't use, and I'll get four dollars back. Guess it will take a while to get a refund since I had to send the ticket to Wilmington, N.C.

I haven't been to Mom's yet. I'll probably wait until Sunday when Pearl can go with me. Farris will be in school until Saturday.

I told Pearl that it looks like Nicky Junior is on the way. She is excited, and she can't understand my doubts . . . .

Tonight I heard the Spotlight Band on the radio; they played one of our favorite numbers, "Brazil."

All my love,

Opal

February 19, 1943

Nicky Darling,

Today I walked from Pearl's to Five Points. I saw Mrs. Madden in the cleaners, and she called to see if Ms. Whitten was home. Georgette and Lama were there, so they walked down the hill to meet me. We hugged and kissed right there on the street. Then we walked to the apartment house and Ms. Whitten made coffee for us. Everyone said to tell you "Hello." The girls want me to move back into the apartment house, but I told them that "The Old Man" won't let me live alone anymore.

Every night about 8:30 or 9:00, I listen for your footsteps at the door. I wish with all my heart that I could open the door and see you standing there.

I Love You,

Opal

February 20, 1943

Darling Opal,

I'm writing from the service club, and the Victrola is playing "I Cried for you." I miss you so much I could cry. I haven't been to Mrs. Jetton's to get my clothes. I'll go tomorrow. I haven't been downtown since you left. I have no reason to go if you are not there. I haven't written to you in so long that I've forgotten what to say.

I'm sorry you had a hard trip home. I wish I had been there to take care of you. I'm also sorry you had a problem with your legs and feet. Darling, stay off your feet and get plenty of rest.

Your Mama's birthday is next month, so let me know what she needs, and we'll buy it. Tell Farris thanks for the nice letter. Thanks for the Beville's lotion; I'm sure it will help. My cold is worse than ever. I need you to take care of me. Last night I received bad news. I can't transfer, but I am going to try for O.C.S. again. Maybe I'll make it this time.

Always yours,
Nicky

February 20, 1943
Darling,

Mom and Dad have moved from the country to Irondale, a little town just outside Birmingham. I am visiting them for a few days. They lived here before, and they have brothers and sisters here. This house is much better than the place in the country. It is old, but sound. It is made of heart pine. It has a nice living room, a large kitchen, three big bedrooms, a bathroom, and a front porch.

The house is right behind the Baptist Church, so Mom can walk there in just a minute or two. The house is only a block from the bus line and near the grocery store, drug store, and post office.

I was glad to see Mom, Dad, and Dot. Everyone is anxious to meet you. I brought your picture with me and showed it to everyone. When Mom saw it, she said you are very handsome. While I was talking to the folks, Freddie came in. He has grown, and he is good-looking. Now that we're all together, we'll make pictures, and I'll send you some.

Darling, yesterday I went to the doctor, and he said I am about three months pregnant. What do you think, Honey? I know we said we wanted to wait until after the war to start a family, but it looks like Little Nicky is on the way. If he is like you, I will love him.

Always and forever,
Opal

February 22, 1943
Nicky Darling,

I'm anxious to hear from you. I left you a week ago, and it seems like a year. I've written every day, and if I don't get a letter from you soon, I think I'll go crazy. I go to the mailbox twenty times a day.

I want more than anything to come back to North Carolina to the dearest boy I know. I didn't think I'd be so lonesome with all the folks around, but all I can think about is you. Sometimes I don't hear what people say to me.

Love always,

Opal

February 24, 1943

Nicky Darling,

I've written you thirteen letters, and I've received only one. What is wrong? I know you would write if you could.

The weather here is nice, but the temperature tonight will be twenty-two degrees. It gets cold here, but it doesn't stay cold long. Mom says spring is just around the corner.

I will keep writing. I know that mail will be forwarded if you are transferred. I am lonely. There is a place in my heart that only you can fill.

I love you,

Opal

February 25, 1943

Nicky Darling,

How is my Sweetheart tonight? I am hoping and praying that you are well and safe. It has been ages since I heard from you . . . .

Emmett got a job at the airplane factory. He and Pearl are grateful.

I'm blue, and I don't feel like talking to anyone. I love you so much. Life without you would mean nothing.

Always,

Opal

February 26, 1943

Nicky Darling,

What's wrong with my husband? Why hasn't he written to me? When I don't hear from you, I worry constantly—you may be sick, you may have been transferred, you may have found another girl. I am not leaving the house today. I am staying here and waiting for the postman.

I love you,

Opal

February 26, 1943

Darling Opal,

Sorry you had to wait so long for a letter. I haven't written because last Sunday I went to the dispensary and I had a fever of 101 degrees. I went to the hospital, and I didn't get out until noon today.

Robbins [one of the soldiers of B Company] just came in to see me, and as usual, he's doing all the talking. He talks a lot but he doesn't say much. I'm pretending to listen as I write. I am lost without you. If I make it to O.C.S., I will go to Fort Benning, and that will be grand.

Darling, I know I told you I didn't want to have children until after the war, but I'm glad we're going to have a baby. We'll manage somehow. I hate to think you will go through pain and hardship and I may not be there.

I miss having my arms around you. I miss lying close to you. I even miss your cold feet against my back.

Your husband,
Nicky

February 28, 1943
Nicky Darling,

I am at Pearl's. I was happy and relieved this morning when Pearl came into the kitchen and handed me a letter from you. I'm so sorry you still have a cold. You're sick because I'm not there to keep you covered up at night.

I do hope you can go to O.C.S.; maybe then you could be assigned closer to Birmingham.

Mom liked the pillow tops. She showed them to everyone and said, "This is what my son-in-law sent me." I told her you picked them out yourself.

Did the Beville's Lotion help your feet? I hope so.

As for finances, I have about six dollars. I am giving Pearl a dollar a day for groceries. I'll send you money as soon as I get a check. If you need money now, I'll borrow from Daddy and send it right away.

Today on the radio, I heard "The Army Hour" broadcasting from Pope Field at Fort Bragg. Reporters inside one of the large planes described how paratroopers get set to jump. I know you boys take risks, so please be careful. Last night, I kissed your picture before I went to bed, and then on the radio I heard, "I Just Kissed Your Picture Goodnight." One of my favorite songs is "There are Such Things." If you hear it, think of me.

Love always,
Opal

February 28, 1943
Darling Opal,

I'm sorry you had to wait so long for a letter, but I'm doing the best I can. I'm still recovering from a cold, and we worked hard all week. Tomorrow we jump, and we have a busy week coming up.

Even though you're eating for two, you should watch your weight. Isn't that what Dr. Scott said? I hope our baby is a little girl who looks just like you.

Always thinking of you,
Nicky

March 1943

While Nicky continued training in Fayetteville and Opal resumed life with her family in Birmingham, Allied air forces hit targets in Berlin and Hamburg.

During an air raid alert in London, 173 people were killed in a stampede. Most died of suffocation. No bombs fell into the area.

Strikes in Italy brought war production to a halt.

In March, the entire 101st Airborne Division participated in ten-day maneuvers in the Southern Pines area of North Carolina. March 22 through 24, the 502nd put on a demonstration for Anthony Eden, Foreign Minister of England. May 23 through 28, the 101st continued training with maneuvers near Camden, South Carolina. Planes and gliders transported troops and equipment, and paratroopers jumped over the target area.

Maneuvers were dangerous, and the daring paratroopers sometimes took unnecessary risks. The first Soldier's Medal awarded in the 101st was given posthumously to Lt. Thomas E. Parlaman. Parlaman dived into the Middle River to rescue a glider infantryman who fell from a raft. The infantryman drifted to safety, but Parlaman drowned. The second Soldier's Medal was awarded to Lt. Robert G. Goodall of the Medical Company. Goodall rescued a trooper who dropped into a pond and was in danger of drowning before he could shed his parachute and equipment. The third Soldier's Medal was awarded to Sgt. George R. Puflett of the 506th for a similar rescue.

★ ★ ★ ★ ★ ★ ★ ★ ★ ★ ★ ★ ★

March 1, 1943
Nicky Darling,

I was thrilled to hear from you. I'm so sorry you've been sick. I knew something was wrong. I thought you might have been transferred. I wish I could be there to take care of you. If I had known you were in the hospital, I would have come right away. That night you left, the station was stifling hot, and then you ran out into the cold to catch the bus. That must have made you sick.

I haven't left the house for fear the postman would come while I was gone. The last time I checked the mail, I prayed, "Oh, God in heaven, please let me get some mail today," and my prayer has been answered. I say a prayer for you every night and I hope you will pray for me.

When I was in Fayetteville and you asked me if I had dated anyone, I was hurt. Since we became engaged, I haven't dated at all, and I have no intentions of dating. I am in love with you; I promised to love, honor, and cherish you, and now my life is yours.

"Little Nicky Boy" will be here at the end of August. I guess it was meant to be, a gift from God. Would you rather have a girl? I can stay with Mom and Dad, and it will cost only about $85 to have the baby at the hospital. If you're still in the States, I want to be with you. Maybe I could have the baby at an army hospital. You're boss, and I'll do what you say. I told Georgette and Lama about the baby, and they are happy for us.

The weather here has been chilly, and I have a cold. Coffee is rationed. One pound is supposed to last six weeks. I have ration book No. 2 now.

Everyone says I've gotten fat, that married life must agree with me.

Love always,

Opal and Little Nicky

March 3, 1943

Hello Darling,

It's twenty-one degrees outside, and snow is on the ground. Mom and Dad's house is cold. They have two fireplaces and a coal-fired heater, but I got used to steam heat in the apartment house, and I'm freezing.

Do I need to save for income tax? Money goes so quickly. What would you think about me going back to work? Maybe then, I could save a little every payday.

I miss your scratchy beard and your warm body; I miss pulling the covers over you and watching you fall asleep. I miss waking up at 4:10 A.M. and trying to help you get ready to go to camp. I know I was just in the way. I miss waiting all day to hear your footstep on the porch and your hand on the doorknob. I miss your laugh. I miss a thousand things about being with you.

Love always,

Opal and Little Nicky

March 4, 1943

Nicky Darling,

I'm at Pearl's. It was eighteen degrees last night. Today, Pearl and I washed some clothes and hung them on the line to dry. When we brought them in, they were frozen stiff. We had to dry them on racks in front of the radiator. It is raining and snowing tonight.

My brother James had an operation for a stomach ulcer. The army hospital sent us a telegram saying that he is in a serious condition.

Sometimes you have trouble with your stomach, so be careful what you eat, and don't drink whiskey. A beer or two is okay, but whiskey is not good for you. Now, don't think I'm trying to be boss; I just want you to take care of yourself.

I've gained some weight in the bust, and my clothes are tight in the waist. One day I was sick, but that's all the trouble I've had from "Little Nicky."

I'm always building air castles for us. When the war is over, we will live in a nice little house, and I'll stay home and take care of you and the baby. I know we will be happy

Haven't been to the movies. Most of the ones playing in Birmingham are pictures we saw in Fayetteville, "Casablanca," "White Cargo," "Tarzan," and "Reveille with Beverly."

New jobs open up every day in Birmingham. Emmett likes his job at the airport. I could get a job if you would not mind me working for a few months.

Loving you,

Opal and Junior

March 4, 1943

My Darling Wife,

We came back from the field about 3:00 P.M. It was terrible out there. When we started, it was drizzling. Later rain began pouring. Then it turned cold. We were soaked to the skin. We couldn't build fires. However, we are back, and I haven't been transferred. Payday is tomorrow, and I'll send you and Junior some money.

Always yours,

Nicky

March 4, 1943

Nicky Darling,

Sweetheart, my brother James is very sick. He's at the Schneck Memorial Hospital in Seymour, Indiana. The hospital sent three telegrams. The last one asked someone to come at once, so Daddy rode the train up there. We're all worried but we're hoping that James will pull through.

Honey, I know you don't like the food in camp, but eat plenty of fruits and vegetables. I think army food made James sick.

I Love You.

Opal

March 5, 1943

Hi Opal Darling,

The company went on a hike at 2:30 P.M. today, but I didn't have to go. The boys will stay out all night and tomorrow, but I am working with the supply. We have a radio in the supply room , and I'm listening to Benny Goodman's "Where or When." Do you remember that piece?

Last night I went to the Villanova. I ate antipasto and a plate of spaghetti. I drank three cups of coffee, and then I went straight back to camp.

The Captain and I are still on the warpath. He doesn't want me to go to O.C.S. He is doing everything he can to keep me here. He says he can't afford to let me go. I don't believe that.

I am pleased about the baby. If it is a boy, he will be a champ, and if it is a girl, she will be beautiful. Darling, please be careful. Don't wrestle with Farris like you used to.

Say, Honey, tell Emmett that when I come down there, he and I are going to go out and have a beer.

Don't forget to buy a birthday present for Mom. Tell her I love her, even though I haven't met her. I love her because she is the mother of my wonderful wife.

Forever yours,

Nicky

March 6, 1943

Nicky Darling,

Are you well? You said you were going into the field. Was it cold there? You should not have been out so soon after having a fever of 101 degrees.

We've had rain for a few days. We haven't heard from Daddy, but we hope James is better. Don't know any news.

It's Saturday, and if I were in Fayetteville, you would be getting off work early, and we would be together until Monday morning.

I have been thinking about the day I was packing to leave. You were lying on the bed resting. I looked at you, and I thought, "This may be the last time I will ever see my Nicky Boy." I wanted to lie down beside you, and I wanted time to stop.

Love always,

Opal

March 6, 1943

Dearest Opal,

How's my best girl? How's Junior? Is the little rascal kicking yet? I got a letter from Farris. Tell him his Uncle Nicky was asking for him.

I'm working in the supply room again.

Last night I went to town and had my picture taken. I'll get three 3 X 5, black and white pictures for three dollars. I went to the Rainbow, and then I saw "Lucky Jordan" at the Colony. I wish you had been with me.

You promised to make me a cake, and I know I'll get it soon. I can hardly wait.

Your husband,

Nicky

March 7, 1943

Dear Opal,

Sorry I couldn't write last night; I was on guard duty. I miss you making sandwiches for me, kissing me when I leave, and kissing me when I get home.

Tonight at the movie, I saw "Random Harvest," and I wished you were here.

I hate to hear that James is sick, but he is young and strong. He'll come out of surgery fine. I said a prayer for him.

You asked me if it's all right to work. I hardly know what to say. Is it safe for you to work in your condition?

Soon we will be going on maneuvers. Maybe we'll go down to Alabama. We are jumping Wednesday. If I sprained an ankle, I might be sent home to recuperate. Guess I'll have no such luck.

Where, oh where is my cake? Do you know how to make one?

When this stinking war is over, I have big plans for you, Junior, and me. I'll do everything to make you and him proud of me. I know I'll be proud of that kid. Remember, I said I was fighting for you? Now I am fighting for Junior too.

Yours always,
Nicky

March 7, 1943
Nicky Darling,

I'm at Mom's. I spent the night last night, and I'll go back to Pearl's today. Dot's baby Patricia is pretty. She has blue eyes and a fair complexion, but not much hair. Her little fuzz looks like it will be chestnut brown, not as red as Dot's hair and mine. Do you think we will have a pretty baby?

Love always,
Opal

March 8, 1943
My Darling Nicky,

Sweetheart, you didn't have to send me money. Keep your money. I know you like to eat in town and go to the show. What did Mrs. Jetton say when you went to her house to get your clothes? Are Mr. and Mrs. Carr moving into our place? Mrs. Jetton will have a hard time finding roomers better than Sgt. and Mrs. Bonilla. We were very content and very quiet.

I wonder if I'll be jealous of Junior. Will you love him more than you love me? Is it wrong to think such a thing?

I haven't told Mom about the baby. She was so worried about James; I thought I'd wait until we hear better news from him. I know Mama will be thrilled when I tell her. I did tell Dot, and she is happy. She said she would do anything to help. She said I could move to Irondale, live with them, and save some money. Mom, Pearl and Dot are very good to me, but I will never be at home without my

Dot and Patricia Conaway

"Nicky Boy." Come on; get those stripes back. Then I can be with you in Fayetteville.

I'm becoming a cook, a housekeeper, and a mother all at the same time. I want to be the ideal housewife. When we are together in a home of our own, I'll make everything cozy.

James is much better, and Daddy is home. He made a quick trip. Please send James a card or a letter if you find time.

How are your feet? If you run out of Beville's Lotion let me know, and I'll get some more.

All my clothes are too tight, and I'll have to buy some maternity dresses. Guess I'll get Nicky Jr. some cute little clothes. Would you go shopping for baby clothes, or would you be embarrassed?

You are a wonderful husband, and you will be a fine "Papa" for Nicky Jr. You are the finest man I have ever met.

Love you always,
Opal

James Keith at Schneck Memorial Hospital, Seymour, Indiana, 1943.

March 9, 1943
Nicky Darling,

I had an argument with Pearl and Emmett tonight. I want to pay them room and board, but they don't want to take my money. I told them they would have to, or I would move out to Mom's. Emmett finally agreed to take four dollars a week.

Daddy came to see us today. He made the trip to Indiana in eleven hours and the trip back to Birmingham in ten hours. He rode the Streamliner. Daddy is a Mason, and the ticket agent was a Mason, so he helped Daddy get on the express train. There was ice and snow in Indiana, but Daddy liked the weather. He says James is getting excellent treatment.

Freddie was working at a hand grenade plant, but now he is working at the Southern Railway shop. He is a smart kid, and he'll have a good chance for advancement.

Daddy is going to plant a garden, and this summer Mom will can vegetables. They are also going to get some rabbits, and keep them in a pen in the back yard. Mom has a rooster and twelve hens. The hens lay ten to eighteen eggs a day. Mom's eggs are much better than those people buy at the store.

I love you, miss you, and wish you were here.

Opal

March 11, 1943

Nicky Darling,

Yes, I'm going to make a cake for you, but I have to wait until sugar stamp Number 12 can be used. Don't even think about twisting an ankle, not even as a joke! I want to see you, but I don't want you to get hurt. Please be careful!

I've clipped many newspaper and magazine pictures and stories for our scrapbook. In one of them, the Brigadier General of Fort Benning is reviewing Canadian paratroopers before they make a mass jump . . . .

Love,

Opal and Junior

March 11, 1943

Dearest Opal,

I'm sorry you had to wait so long for a letter. In a few days, we will go on maneuvers, and we've been working constantly to get everything ready. Monday night we went to radio school and Tuesday night we cleaned our parachutes.

The married boys are sending their wives home, and they are the most sorrowful bunch you have ever seen. I know exactly how they feel. When you left, I lost something that I will not find until we are together again.

Last night I ate at the Brass Rail Cafe and I drank a couple of glasses of wine. Then I went to see James Cagney in "Yankee Doodle Dandy." Darling, don't miss it. It is excellent

I'm glad your family is happy that we are having a baby! I wouldn't be embarrassed to buy baby clothes. In fact, I think I'd enjoy it.

I keep pestering the Captain to give me a three-day pass. Maybe he'll get tired of seeing me and hearing me, and he'll give me a pass just to get rid of me. Since I was busted, I lost my room, and I sleep out in the barracks with the rest of the men, but I have your picture hanging by my bed. I'm looking at it, and I've concluded that you are a gorgeous girl.

Hey Pug, do you still wear my wings when you go out? Been to the movies? You should go out every once is a while and have a little fun. Lights off in a few minutes.

Forever yours,

Nicky

March 12, 1943
Nicky Darling,

How's my soldier boy tonight? It's raining here, but it's not cold. I'll be so glad when summer comes. Remember how hot it was last summer? We sat in the back booth at Romeo's near the kitchen, and we almost died of the heat? We didn't care. All we wanted was to be together.

Do you think you might go to O.C.S.? Do you want to? If I thought you could stay in the U.S., I'd be glad for you to go. If you ever think you're leaving Fort Bragg, and if you know where you're going, tell me. Then I won't worry about you so much, and I will not tell anyone.

Mrs. Bonilla has quite an appetite these days, but I'm eating well—fresh fruits and vegetables, milk and eggs. Nicky Jr. may be a big boy, eight or nine pounds.

I'm waiting for the postman, and he'd better have some mail for me. If he doesn't, I'm going to yell real loud . . . .

All my love,
Opal

March 13, 1943
My Darling Opal,

Tonight I'm on guard. I just came off duty, and I'll go on again at 6:00 A.M. I work until 10:00 A.M., and then I'm off for the weekend . . . .

One day this week, I drove to town to get supplies. When I got back, it was too late for dinner. The cook said, "If you want to eat, you'll have to cook it yourself." I fried six eggs, three slices of ham, made four pieces of toast, ate half a can of fruit salad, and drank three cups of coffee. That is the biggest meal I've eaten since you left. You've been gone four weeks, and it seems like four years. But, I can't squawk too much; I have a wonderful wife, and we are going to have a son.

Did you buy Mom a hat? Did she like it? Are you really going to make me a cake? Don't let Mom cook it and then tell me you did it. I want a cake cooked by you alone.

Always yours,
Nicky

March 13, 1943
My Darling Wife,

Wednesday is Saint Patrick's Day. In New York, the Irish will dress in green and wear shamrocks. They'll parade through the streets with bagpipers playing, and they'll be very proud of themselves. I'm always proud of my Irish girl. Here is an Irish blessing for you.

May you be blessed
with the strength of Heaven,
the light of the sun,

the radiance of the moon,
the splendor of fire,
the speed of lightening,
the swiftness of wind,
the depth of the sea,
the stability of the earth
and the firmness of rock."

[From The Breastplate of St. Patrick, traditional Irish poetry translated by C. F. Alexander.]

A paratrooper from the 504th was killed. He had a military funeral. His flag-draped casket rested on a caisson, a wagon for hauling ammunition, pulled by horses. The Regiment marched behind. The band played, the bugler blew taps, and a rifle squad fired three volleys. It was so sad that some of the boys cried.

Today I received a letter from a boy in Africa. He was shot in the leg, and he is in the hospital over there.

Here on the post I saw "Forever and a Day." It had as many stars as "Star Spangled Rhythm." Right now, I'm listening to the radio playing "Brazil." It is Number One on the Hit Parade. Tomorrow we go to the field for a couple of days.

Sometimes I am sorry that I met you because I'm in such misery when we're apart. Now the radio is playing "Blue Moon." It describes me exactly: "Without a dream in my heart, without a love of my own." Another number I like is "At Last." Glen Miller plays that piece very well.

I'm going to church tomorrow morning, and I'll say a prayer for you, James, and the family.

Yours forever and a day,
Nicky

March 14, 1943
Nicky, Darling,

I'm at Mom's; the sun is shining bright, and it's nice and warm. If you were here, we could go to the movies this evening. I haven't been to the show since you and I went together. I don't care to go if I can't go with you. Would you believe it; the radio is playing "Don't Get Around Much Anymore."

I showed Mom, Daddy, Dot, and Freddie your new picture, and they said that you are a fine-looking man. Mom is very pleased about Junior.

Love always,
Opal and Junior

March 15, 1943
Nicky Darling,

Monday, Mom and I went to town, and I bought her a hat, $6.12. It is a black sailor style with white flowers on the brim and a pretty veil. It looks good on her, and she loves it. She appreciates you wanting to give her a birthday present. I bought her a pair of stockings and a birthday card. Daddy got her some flowers to plant.

Mom is going to stay with Pearl for a few days, and I'm staying with Dot. Dot's baby, Patricia, is a doll. She is seven months old and very active. She rolls, scoots, and crawls everywhere.

We got a telegram from James. He sent it himself, and he says he is "improving day by day."

Mom got your letter. When you wrote "Dear Mom," and signed, "Your Son," you made her very happy. She wants you to feel like you are her own son. Daddy thinks well of you because you care for me. I haven't told him about Junior.

Should we tell your mother about the baby? I wish your family would accept me as my family has accepted you. If your mother only knew how much I love you.

Before I get too big to travel, I'd like to come to Fayetteville. I wouldn't care if I could stay only a few days. Do I have time to visit before you go on maneuvers?

Love always,
Opal

March 15, 1943
My Darling Opal,

I came back from the field at 3:30 P.M. It wasn't too bad out there. We didn't have to walk all night. We rested until 6:00 A.M., and then we attacked an enemy position. When I got in, I was very tired, so I slept until 5:30 P.M. Then I went to the Service Club, ate supper, and saw a movie.

Do you want me to send Butch to you? Would you like to have a puppy? Maybe you don't want the responsibility of caring for a dog. Let me know.

Say Honey, your birthday is coming around, and I haven't the slightest idea what to buy for you. Will you give me a hint? Now, don't tell me not to buy you a gift. I want to give you something nice.

I ate in town tonight: two small steaks, $1.00; two orders of French fried potatoes, 20 cents; cooked apples, 15 cents; a piece of pie, 10 cents, and 4 cups of coffee, 5 cents for a total of $1.50. I can't eat that damned canned beans and meat. Remember, I brought you some to try, and it was awful.

I wish you could come up here for a short visit, but you probably shouldn't travel. Trains and buses are too crowded and unpredictable. I'll have to come down there.

Tell Pearl and Emmett that I appreciate everything they do for you. Give my love to the family.

Love always,
Nicky

March 16, 1943
Dearest Opal,

How are you tonight? Today was an easy day. This morning we played baseball, and this afternoon we got ready for a couple more days in the field. We leave here tomorrow morning and stay out until Friday or Saturday.

The 517th will be activated on April 14, and I may be chosen to train the new men. The rumor is that the outfit is going to Alabama. I'm going to work hard and hope I make it. But don't get too excited; it's not definite.

I ate dinner at the service club. I love the coffee they make. I buy one cup and get all the free refills I want. I think I'll go to see "Frankenstein and the Wolfman." I don't think a woman in your condition should see a picture like that.

Last night I heard Dr I.Q. on the radio. One of the ladies who won silver dollars was from Irondale. The rest of the contestants were from Birmingham. What is it like in Irondale? Do people still gossip like they did when you lived there before? How's Junior? Is he treating you well? Would you like to have twins? Then you would be the talk of the town.

I'm seriously thinking about growing a moustache. Do you think it would make me look old?

I will always love you,
Nicky

March 16, 1943
Hello, Nicky Darling,

I'm at Mom's, it is 5:30 A.M., and I'm up. What does my Tootsie think of that? Freddie, my little brother, has to catch the bus to town at 5:30, so Dot and I got up and cooked his breakfast. Dot is a darn good cook. You should taste the rolls she makes. Since coffee is rationed, we drink coffee with chicory. It's good and strong. There was an empty place at the table, and I wished you were sitting there smiling at me.

I think I will stay with Mom and Dad until you and I get a place of our own. There is more room here than at Pearl's apartment, and Mom and Dot need all the help they can get to take care of everyone.

Freddie is working at Southern Railway as a storehouse clerk. He is an apprentice, but he has a good chance for advancement. He is making fifty-four cents an hour.

Patricia, Dot's baby, is the main attraction here. She smiles, coos, pulls her booties off, and sticks her toes in her mouth. Sometimes she will reach out and grab a handful of my hair.

We haven't been to the movies. I wanted to see Ethyl Barrymore in "The Corn is Green," but I didn't want to go alone. You would be surprised at how few cars are on the streets. Everyone rides buses and streetcars, and people are packed in. Last time I went to town, I stood for the whole trip, seven miles, and it took about an hour to travel that far. The fellows on the buses aren't gentlemanly like you.

They don't stand to give a lady a seat.

James is almost well, and he has a good appetite. He wants Mom to send him some grits. Ha. Ha. He asked for grits at the hospital, but nobody knew what they were. He will be at Schneck Memorial Hospital for another week. Then, they'll send him to an army hospital until he is able to come home.

Dad is working as a watchman at a war plant.

I'm going to make a cake for you one day this week. I warn you, it's been a long time since I've baked, so the cake might not taste very good.

Was the photographer who made your picture a pretty girl? You sure are smiling for someone. Is that smile just for me? I thought so.

Love always,

Opal

March 17, 1943

Nicky Darling,

How is my husband today? I've put all the clippings and pictures you sent in the scrapbook, and Mom and I looked at it. She says it must be dangerous to be a paratrooper.

My cousin Minnie and her husband came to visit from Bessemer. Minnie and Frank think you're good-looking, and Frank said your name sounds Italian. They look forward to meeting you.

When you visit, you'll wear your summer uniform? You look good in anything you wear, but I want to see you in civilian clothes. I'm going to make that cake tomorrow since sugar stamp Number 12 was not valid until Saturday. We've already used our supply of Number 11 stamps.

I was with you in Fayetteville only a short time. I was just beginning to know you. I hated to leave. I pray that we will be together again soon.

Words can't express my love for you.

Opal

March 18, 1943

My Darling Nicky Boy,

How's the best soldier in the Army? Are you going to bring Butch here from New York? I'd like to have him and a cute puppy for my birthday. I'll take good care of Butch. I don't have anything else to do.

I enjoy being here with the folks. I told Mom about Junior, but I can't get up the courage to tell Dad. He'll know soon enough, but I still don't show. The doctor told me it probably happened on December 25. What a Christmas present! Nicky Jr. will be here about the middle of September.

When we were together, I could never tell you how much I love you. It seems that I can say more in letter. I hope you feel my love for you as I feel your love for me.

Yours always,

Opal

March 19, 1943
Nicky Darling,

Oh! Gee! I do hope you come to Alabama to help train the new men. Try hard to get along with the Captain so he'll let you go. I can't help being excited. To have you near would be wonderful. We could get a little apartment somewhere, and you could come home to me every night. As far as I'm concerned, they can give Irondale back to the Indians. I want to be with you.

When I was in Fayetteville, we were beginning to get used to each other's little faults. I know that my feelings are hurt too easy. Some wife! A big crybaby. But I'll try not to be so sensitive.

I don't know how I feel about you growing a mustache. I don't think you'd look good with one, but let it grow and see how it looks.

Love always,
Opal

March 20, 1943
My Darling Nicky,

This afternoon I made your cake, and I mailed it. It's been a long time since I baked, so if the cake is lopsided, don't be surprised. The next one will be better.

Honey, the airplane factory in Birmingham is hiring lots of people. Even schoolgirls are working in the daytime and going to classes three nights a week. What would you think about me working for a few months?

Dot and I thought about going to a movie, but it has rained all night. Another Saturday night without you.

I love you,
Opal

March 20, 1943
Opal Darling,

I just came in from the field and found five letters waiting for me. You know, mail is important to soldiers. Nothing builds morale like letters from home.

In the field, we walked 50 or 60 miles, and I'm tired, but I didn't want to keep you waiting for a letter. I can think of nothing but you and Junior. Do you have enough money? Do you need another maternity dress? Check with Mrs. Whitten to see if she has war bonds for you. And let me know if you received the insurance policy.

I am glad James has improved enough to come home. When James asked for grits at the hospital, I will bet they thought he was crazy. Up North, they don't know what grits is. They don't even know what cornbread is. I didn't know what they were until I came south. Now that I'm half Rebel, I've learned to like Southern cooking.

Is it getting warm there? I think I'll put my overcoat in storage until next winter. Maybe I'll never need it again. I'll be a civilian trying to support a family. I love my wife, and I could shout it from the top of the world.

Say Honey, I have about twenty cans of that powdered coffee. You liked it, so I'll send it to you. Each can makes a quart.

I wish you could come up here, but now is not the time; we are going on maneuvers soon. Save some money, and when I get time off, you can come flying. I might go on furlough at the end of April. Maybe we can find an inn in the country where we can be alone.

Glad you liked the picture. I smiled my best smile for my best girl.

Yours always,
Nicky

March 21, 1943
Dearest Opal,

Know what today is? The first day of spring. But it has been raining, and it's cold. Luckily, the barracks are nice and warm.

I got a nice letter from Dot. I'm waiting for my cake. I will taste my wife's cooking very soon. Speaking of cooking, dinner tonight was lousy: hash, boiled potatoes, beets, cocoa, bread and butter, and ice cream. I should have gone to the service club, but it was raining too hard.

I'm listening to the radio as I write, and Harry James is playing "Stardust." Pretty, isn't it? I love you.

Always,
Nicky

March 23, 1943
My Darling Nicky Boy,

Did you get your cake? Was it mashed? If you like it, I'll send something else, maybe a pie. Do you like apple?

I'll be so glad if you get a furlough. We'll find a nice quiet place where we can be together and forget the worries of the world.

I bought a maternity dress. It is navy blue silk with light blue, pink, and white flowers with green stems. It was $11.17. I haven't worn it yet. It seems so large, and I'm not going to wear it until I have to.

I saw Dr. Scott, the baby doctor. He is old and very nice. He weighed me, listened to my heart, and checked my blood pressure. I weigh 137 pounds. He gave me a diet so I won't gain weight too fast. I paid him $9.00 for three visits.

Have you written to your mother? Does she write to you? You mentioned getting Butch from her and sending him to me. I really don't think you should. There is too much going on here; he might not get the best care.

Mom and Dad are very kind to all of us. They won't let me spend a penny. Now I should be able to save some money.

This afternoon, Dot and a girlfriend are going to town to see "The Meanest Man in the World" at the Alabama Theater. I'll stay home and take care of Patricia. She is cute, but she has the Keith Irish temper. She cries for someone to hold her all the time. I told Mom, "If Nicky Jr. is bad, I'll spank him," and Mom said, "No you won't; I'll see to that. I'll spoil him just as we've spoiled this baby." Taking care of Patricia keeps us occupied, and I'm getting experience that I'll need when our baby comes. You know, Hon, it's going to be a shock if Nicky Jr. is a girl. I've counted on having a little boy just like you.

James is anxious to come home. He told Mom to throw the feed to the flock, because he'll be ready for one of her chicken dinners. Often Mom or Dad says, "I wish my sons were home," and they consider you one of their sons. Maybe the war will be over soon, and we will be together.

I'll love you always,

Opal

Chapter Three

Training for an Invasion: Birmingham and Fayetteville

As Opal learned to cook and prepared for the birth of her baby, Nicky participated in maneuvers near Camden, South Carolina. These maneuvers were staged to prepare the men of the 101st for the Tennessee Maneuvers, full-scale war games. Troopers flew to drop zones on transport planes and jumped. Gliders were cut loose over the target area. Vehicles and artillery were in short supply, but locations of tanks and big guns were simulated. Troopers began to see what airborne fighting was all about.

★ ★ ★ ★ ★ ★ ★ ★ ★ ★ ★ ★ ★

March 23, 1943
Dearest Opal,

A.M. Today George Marshall, the Chief of Staff, is visiting camp. Our battalion is staging a battle for him, and we're firing the ammunition. I may get a furlough after that.

P.M. We staged our battle today, but General Marshall never did come. He is coming tomorrow, for sure, and we have to go through the whole thing again. Yesterday it snowed hard for half an hour, and I could hardly see my hand in front of my face. Then the snow stopped, and the weather began to warm up.

Thursday we go on maneuvers for seven or eight days. Please continue to write, and I'll get your letters when I return to camp. I'll write every day if I can and mail all the letters at once if I have to. I haven't heard anything about going to the new outfit. So long, and stay as sweet as you are.

Remember Sadie Hawkins, the kid you met in front of the theater one night? He sleeps next to me, and if I catch him looking at your picture, I make him bow his head and say, "I'm sorry I allowed my profane eyes to rest on your divine beauty, Mrs. Bonilla. Please forgive me."

I love you.
Nicky

March 24, 1943
Nicky Darling,

Don't write to me when you're tired. Sleep first, and then write.

You asked about rationing. We get one pound of coffee that has to last five weeks. Five pounds of sugar has to last five or six weeks. There is almost no candy or gum. Cases in stores used to be filled with candy, but now they display small cakes, nuts, and crackers. I asked all the churchgoers about whiskey rationing, and they claimed not to know anything about it

I am considering having my hair cut short and getting a permanent wave. What do you think?

The crystal came off my watch, and I lost it. I spent seventy-five cents to replace it. But I didn't care what it cost. I love my watch because you gave it to me when we were married.

Always yours,
Opal and Junior

March 24, 1943
Dear Opal,

Darling, today I'm the happiest man alive. I tasted my wife's cooking for the first time! That was the most delicious cake I've ever eaten. How did you know that I like coconut? I ate half of the cake with powdered coffee, and then I passed the rest around the barracks. I told the boys that my wife made the cake. I threw out my chest and strutted around like the cock of the walk. I can hardly wait for the next cake. I wish you were with me so you could cook for me all the time. With your cooking and your loving, I would live in bliss.

We put on that battle for the big shots today. General Marshall, President Roosevelt and Mrs. Roosevelt; Madame Chiang Kai Shek; Anthony Eden, ambassador from England; and several English and French generals were here. By the way, some boys in the 504th are leaving next week. That's the outfit with the A. A. insignia. So long until I can write again.

Always yours,
Nicky

March 25, 1943
My Darling Opal,

Today we went down to Pope Field, boarded a plane, and made a jump. We attacked an airport about 50 miles away. Of course, we captured it. Now we're in camp. I'm writing from my tent. I have a candle fixed inside a shiny can, and it gives good light. All the boys asked me how I thought of that, and I told them that a good soldier always comes prepared.

Have to close now; blackout.

I Love You,
Nicky

March 27, 1943
Darling Opal,

Didn't write yesterday because we were away from base camp where our tents are. We were fighting a battle and were on the go all the time. Couldn't build fires or smoke cigarettes because the enemy might see the light and know where we were.

The last battle was fun. The 401st Glider Infantry was our enemy. We attacked them at 6:00 A.M., and we kept pushing them back until we wiped them out. I captured 3 Jeeps and 16 men. I put food and water in one of the jeeps and I went after the enemy. In fact, I did not see B Company for days. I even found a small town and had a bath in a barbershop. The barber charged me fifty cents.

It's evening, and I'm wearing my heavy underwear, two pairs of socks, a wool cap, and my overcoat. My hands are cold, but I don't care. I want to write to you. If I were at the North Pole, I would still write to my sweet wife.

When I come to Alabama, are you going to cook a meal for me? All by yourself? Darling, don't drink too much coffee. It might hurt Junior.

Your husband,
Nicky

Opal, Emmett, Pearl and Farris.

March 27, 1943
My Darling Nicky,

When you're in the field and can't write, I miss your letters. Mom and Pearl will want us to stay with them when you come on furlough, but let's get a room where we can be alone. I miss having a place of my own. My clothes are scattered everywhere. I wish I could live in a little apartment in a private home. But all I really want is to be with you.

Did you write to your mother about Nicky Jr.? I wonder if she would be happy to know that she is going to be a grandmother. I weigh 140 pounds. I've gained only four pounds.

Today is sunny, and warm. I've been walking Patricia. She is a sweet baby, but when she starts crying, I give her to Dot or Mom.

I'll love you always,
Opal

March 28, 1943
Dear Opal,

How are you Darling? When I got up this morning, it was so cold I didn't go to breakfast; I stayed in bed until mail call at 11:00 A.M. I got two letters and pictures. This is probably the last letter I'll write until Thursday, so if you don't hear

Nicky and his squad. Nicky is kneeling third from left.

from me, don't worry. . . .

Would you like me to send you some candy and gum? I can buy all I want in camp.

Mom said she will send me a cake. I wonder if it will be better than the one you sent. You know, she is an experienced cook. I love you.

Always yours,

Nicky

March 28, 1943

Nicky Darling,

Thank you for the cheerful letters. I know I shouldn't complain. I don't mean to make you blue, but sometimes I feel frustrated. I hardly ever have a minute to myself, and you're the only one I want to spend time with.

We wanted to make pictures Sunday, but the little drugstore here in Irondale had no film. We'll have to go to Woodlawn or Birmingham to buy film.

The grass is green and jonquils are blooming in the yard. Soon we'll have warm weather. Now I won't be such a house rat. I've been walking with Patricia. She loves to be outside. She's beginning to talk. She says, "Mama."

Wouldn't it be grand if we could be together all summer, dancing, swimming, and playing tennis? Someday we'll do everything we want to do.

Have you been to the Highland Cafeteria? I haven't eaten spaghetti since I've been here. And I've had no wine or beer. Mom is a teetotaler, so I'll wait to drink a glass of wine with you.

We cooked a vegetable supper this evening. Fred went to the store to get meat, but we forgot to give him ration book Number 2, and he wouldn't go back. Our meal was good even without meat.

After supper, we listened to a play, "Crossroads," on the Lux Radio Theater.

Every night I say a special prayer for you.

Always yours,

Opal

March 31, 1943

Hello Darling,

I laughed when you said you've been wearing long handled drawers. I'd like to see you in that outfit. I'm glad you're dressing warmly.

Thanks for offering to send candy and gum, but I eat too much as it is. You're generous to offer.

Today Fred and I played catch with a softball. I'm teaching Nicky Jr. to be a champion. I know you will love him, but if you love him more than you love me, I think I'll be a little jealous.

I'm saving money so we can go out when you come down here. Cocktail lounges don't allow dancing, and places where you can dance can't sell beer or whiskey. The Tutwiler Hotel still has a bar, but no dancing is allowed.

All the girls I grew up with are married and have children. One of my friends has a son six years old. In five or six months, I'll be a mother, and I know I'll love our baby.

A boy from Irondale was called before the draft board, but they wouldn't accept him because he was a little overweight. He weighed more than 300 pounds. That's as far as their scale registered. Poor kid.

We're listening to the radio and Tommie Dorsey is playing "I'll Never Smile Again." So many songs seem to be written especially for us.

I love you,
Opal and Little Nicky

April 1943

The Allies bombed the Italian mainland and larger islands.

In Germany, Marshall Hermann Goring, head of the Luftwaffe, ordered all able-bodied Germans to perform air raid duty.

U.S. Bombers hit Antwerp causing great damage and R.A.F. planes raided targets in Germany almost nightly.

Heinrich Himmler, head of the *Schutzstaffel* (S.S.), ordered the massacre of Jews in the Warsaw ghetto. At least 56,000 were to be killed by May 16. Jews revolted against their deportation and they continued to fight until May 16 when the revolt was crushed.

★ ★ ★ ★ ★ ★ ★ ★ ★ ★ ★ ★ ★

April 2, 1943
My Darling Nicky,

Are you well and happy? I didn't write yesterday because Dot, Patricia, Aunt Ida, mom's sister-in-law, and I rode the train to Wattsville, about forty-five miles away. We visited my cousin Annie who has a new baby. Annie said that having a baby is very painful. I thought they put you to sleep when the pain started. Annie said the doctors didn't put her to sleep fast enough. I want to be asleep. I think I'll go to the hospital a day ahead of time and stay there until I'm completely well. What do you think?

Tomorrow we are going to town to see the movie "Random Harvest."

Think you'll get a furlough around the 15th? I can hardly wait. Heard anything about a transfer? I want to go wherever you go if we can afford it. If you are transferred to Alabama, it will be too good to be true.

Love always,
Opal

April 3, 1943
Hello Darling,

Got back from the field, a while ago, went to bed, and slept until dinner. We ate well for a change.

Here's a surprise. Since we worked so hard on maneuvers, we're getting three days off. I'll leave here Tuesday night, arrive Wednesday night, and I have to be back Saturday morning. I'll send a telegram to let you know when to meet the train. Reserve a room for us at the Redmont Hotel.

I appreciate the kisses on your letters, but Wednesday night, I'll be kissing you in person. We'll have a little vino, maybe a lot of vino.

I Love You,
Nicky

April 4, 1943
Dear Nicky,

We are having an air raid drill in Birmingham. Enemy planes will attempt to destroy all war plants. Bombs will be dropped, bags filled with sawdust. Red bags with bright colored streamers will represent incendiaries and high explosives. Yellow and green bags will represent other bombs and gas. All workers must be on the job before 2:00 P.M. Everyone must stay inside . . . .

Thinking about seeing you is a joy.

I love you,
Opal

A steel mill in Brimingham, one of the possible targets of bombs.
Office of War Information

★★★★★★★★★★★★★

Nicky received a furlough and spent a few days in Birmingham with Opal. The couple stayed at the Redmont Hotel. They visited Opal's family in Irondale. Louise Keith cooked a big Sunday dinner for her new son-in-law. She served pork roast, fried chicken, mashed potatoes, field peas, salad, turnip greens, cornbread, biscuits, banana pudding, ambrosia, and sweet tea.

★★★★★★★★★★★★★

April 13, 1943
Dearest Opal,

Sorry I didn't send a telegram as soon as I got back. The office was closed; then we went to the field, and we just returned.

I had a wonderful time with you, and soon we'll have more good times. You looked lovely. Your face was glowing and your eyes were shining. I was shocked to hear that you are upset about having the baby. I thought you really wanted it. Don't worry. Nicky Junior will be a healthy baby, you will love him, and you will be a good mother. Even if I am not there when the baby is born, you will have your family to take care of you. I know if we were together, you would not be so worried. I will always be with you in spirit.

You have a fine family. They treated me like one of their own. When I come back to Birmingham, we will visit them every day. Fred is a little bashful, isn't he? He's cute. But I have a confession to make; Pearl is my favorite. I was glad to meet everyone, especially Mom. She is so good.

The sandwiches Mom made spoiled, but the cake and pie were delicious. Don't tell Mom about the sandwiches; it might hurt her feelings.

Last night I went to the Rainbow; then I went to the U.S.O. and wrote you. I went to the Town Pump, drank a couple of beers, and came back to camp.

The 504th is going across. Civilians can't come onto the post, and nobody in that outfit can leave. I don't know anything else to write except that I will love you. . . .

"Until death do us part."

Nicky

April 13, 1943
My Darling Nicky,

How was your trip to Fort Bragg? I know you rode the train all night, and you must have been very tired. Have you been able to rest?

Emmett appreciates the coveralls you gave him. They fit well, but were a little short. Mom will let the hems down, and they'll be good work clothes. And thanks for all the gum, candy, and coffee. You are very thoughtful.

Please forgive me for crying about having the baby. I don't want to be mean and bad, but I'm afraid to have a baby if you are not here to help me care for it. Can you forgive me? Do you still love me? I want to be a good wife and mother, but I don't know if I can raise a child alone.

Mom and Dot say that some women feel down when they first find out they are expecting, but then when the baby comes, they are very happy. I'm sure I will love Nicky Jr. very much. Maybe it is all for the best. I'm getting big. I can't hold my stomach in any more, so I'll have to start wearing maternity dresses. The doctor told me that I should wear low heel shoes.

I went to Romeo's, and I was glad to see everyone. Evelyn says she and Al are still dating, but Mrs. Romeo doesn't want them to go together. Al gave Evelyn a watch, but she can't wear it at work because Mrs. Romeo might see it.

Evelyn wants Al to quit working at the restaurant and get another job so they can be married. If he marries Evelyn, Al will have to give up his family, and I don't think he will ever do that. I am glad you married me even though your mother disapproved. I hope that one day she will accept me.

Always yours,
Opal

April 15, 1943
Nicky Darling,

This afternoon I made a cake for you. Thought I'd try my hand with chocolate. I don't know how it will taste. I think the frosting is too hard, but maybe not so hard that you can't eat it. I'll try to send you a cake every week.

Last time I was in town, I bought a new hat, one that doesn't make me look so tall. I think you'll like it.

Aunt Hattie, Mom's sister, wants you to visit next time you come to Birmingham.

I love you.
Opal

April 15, 1943
My Darling Wife,

I haven't heard from you in a week and I am worried. Are you sick? Has something happened to Junior? Have you stopped loving me? Have you found someone else? All kinds of fears run through my mind. I will always love you, so no matter what is wrong, tell me.

In about an hour, we're going into the field. I'll be back tomorrow and I am praying that I get a letter from you.

Yours always,
Nicky

April 18, 1943
Nicky Darling,

I'm well and happy. I'm happy because I'm in love with my husband, and I'm going to be a mother. I might have twins. You never know. A boy and a girl. I'll name the boy Nicky Jr., and you can name the girl.

Yesterday, Mom and I rode the streetcar to town, and then to Pearl's. I saw Lama and Georgette. They had been to see "The Moon and Sixpence" with George Sanders, but they didn't like it very much.

Mom stayed at Pearl's, and I went home with Georgette and Lama. Mrs. Whitten was there, and she was glad to see me. I told them about Junior, and they are thrilled. I went back to Pearl's apartment to spend the night.

Lama is getting married soon. She said she might wait until you come to Birmingham so we can have a big party. Lama said she wants to get a baby on the first night she is married. Georgette is not married yet; she and her fiancé are waiting until he finishes officers' school. . . .

I Love You,
Opal

April 18, 1943
My Darling,

Today I received three letters, a cake, and several pictures. Hearing from you takes a load off my mind. Honey, don't ever wait so long to write again. Write to me everyday, even if I'm not here to receive your letters. I'll get them eventually.

The chocolate cake was just as good as the coconut. I guess you do know how to cook. Thank you for the $10. I'll admit I need it, and when I come on furlough, we won't have much money. But we'll be together for nine days . . . .

Of course, I forgive you for crying about expecting a baby we didn't plan for. I know if we were together, you would be happy to start a family . . . .

Honey, I told you that most Italian parents insist on their children marrying someone the parents approve of. If Al loves Evelyn, he should marry her, but I don't think he loves her as much as I love you.

This is a long letter. The writing is small and there is not much space between the lines. HA! HA!

Always yours,
Nicky

April 19, 1943
Nicky Darling,

Hello, Sweetheart. I didn't write because I was waiting for a letter or telegram from you. Now I wish I had written. I promise that from now on I will write every day even if it is just to say, "I Love You." Darling, don't ever think that I've found

someone else. You are the only man I will ever love.
Yours always,
Opal and Junior

April 19, 1943
Dearest Opal,

Here I sit in the guardhouse office. It is quiet and a good place to write. I'll be coming to Birmingham around May 1. I'll probably wear my summer uniform. I wish I could take you to Church on Easter morning. I'm looking forward to seeing you in that new hat. You look very glamorous in the picture.

When I show your pictures to the boys, I say, "Did you know I'm married to a movie actress?" They want to know how an ugly mug like me got such a pretty girl. Then I say in my New York accent, "Poisanality, Kid. Poisanality!" That gets a big laugh.

Late last night I made some powdered coffee and drank it as I ate my last piece of cake.

Lots of Love,
Nicky

Trooper descending in parachute
U. S. Army Signal Corps

April 20, 1943
Nicky Darling,

Mom is at Pearl's, and Dot and I are trying to take her place, but it doesn't seem like home without her. We get Fred off to work at 5:30 A.M. Dad sleeps during the day, and we cook supper for him before he goes in to work at 10:30 P.M. Even though Dad is working, he goes to the post office twice a day to mail my letters and pick up the ones you send me.

Dot went to town, and when she came back, I was sweeping the floor with one arm and holding Patricia in the other. Patricia cries if someone is not holding her all the time. Dot laughed when she saw me.

Mom and I cook dinner, so I'm getting plenty of experience. Won't it be great when we're together in our own home and the world is at peace?

I sent you a little Easter card. It isn't pretty, but it's the best I could find in Irondale. Just wanted you to know I'm thinking of you. I would love to go to church with you on Easter Sunday. I've heard that the service at St. Paul's is beautiful.

I haven't made plans for your furlough. I wish I could think of something interesting, but you know how it is here, not much to do. Of course, we could always visit kinfolks. There are at least a hundred that you haven't met.

If someone had told me a year ago that I would be married and expecting a baby, I'd have said, "No, not me! I'm never going to get married," but we did marry, and I am glad.

I love you,
Opal

April 20, 1943
Dear Opal,

Today I received three letters. Tomorrow morning we will get up at 4:30 A.M., go to the field, and attack a town about the size of Irondale. If I can catch a plane, I'll see you Saturday night.

Are you lonely for your husband? I think I'm the most lonesome man in the company, but I have happy memories of our love.

I'm listening to the Coca-Cola Program, and a band is playing "Easter Parade." Someday you and I will walk down Fifth Avenue on Easter Sunday with our beautiful baby between us.

Goodnight, Darling.
Nicky

April 22, 1943
My Darling Wife,

How are you, Sweet? With a 9-day furlough coming up, I'm so happy I could bust. I showed one of my Lieutenants your picture today. He said you are very pretty and I'm a lucky man. I told him that you married me for my money. Ha! Ha!

Last night I dreamed I was home. I was wearing my uniform, and I said I was going to town to buy civilian clothes. You asked me to wait until you got dressed so you could go with me. I sat in a chair and I looked into the bedroom. I saw you brushing your long shimmering hair, and I smelled your perfume. I hope that dream comes true very soon.

The Captain was sick. He was away for a while, but now he is back. He said, "Who made you sergeant?" I said, "The officer who took your place made me sergeant." He is mad.

Tomorrow is Good Friday, so I'll go to church, and I'll go again on Easter. I'll say a prayer for you, Junior, and all the family. By the way, young lady, don't you think you should go to church every once in a while? It wouldn't hurt.

I love you,
Nicky

April 25, 1943
Nicky Darling,

Happy Easter, Sweetheart. Pearl and Farris came to Mom's to spend the day. Dot bought Farris an Easter basket and she dyed Easter eggs. We hid the eggs in the yard, and he had fun hunting for them. We made pictures of Farris and Patricia. We cooked a ham, English peas, carrots, and mashed potatoes for lunch. Mom made a cake with orange-flavored icing. We wished you were here. I didn't get mail Friday or Saturday. Hope I'll get a letter on Monday.

Love always,
Opal

April 25, 1943
Opal Darling,

Did you have a good Easter Sunday? I got up at 4:30 A.M. to go to Sunrise Service. The weather was bright and warm, and after service, I ate breakfast and went back to bed. I got an Easter card from you and one from your family. I wanted to send cards to "you all," but I haven't been to town, and there are no cards on the post. Tomorrow night we're going into the field.

I hope I will be nearby in September when Junior is born. That kid is going to get the best of everything. You said you are worried that I will love the baby more than I love you. Honey, the baby is you. It is made of you, so if I love the baby, I am loving you.

Your husband,
Nicky

April 26, 1943
Nicky Darling,

Yesterday Dot, Pearl, Farris, and I tried to go to the movies. The streetcars were slow, and we got to the theater about fifteen minutes too late to see the last show. So we went window-shopping. Then we had dinner in Woodlawn.

I saw a paratrooper wearing a field jacket. He was not as good-looking a soldier as my Nicky Boy.

Saturday will be a happy day. Send me a telegram and let me know when you'll arrive. I'll meet you at the station. I'm losing my girlish figure, but I'll wear my new hat and look my best just for you.

Always yours,
Opal

April 27, 1943
Dear Opal,

We came back from the field at 6:00 P.M. The weather was good, and some of the boys went swimming tonight. The captain and I are butting heads. He says I will not be sergeant long. I'm trying to keep my mouth shut. If I argue with him, he might not give me a furlough.

Saturday I went to the airport to see if I could get a plane to Birmingham. Nothing leaving here until Sunday.

Honey, when I come to Alabama, I'll meet all one hundred of those kinfolks at once, if that's what you want me to do. Goodnight.

I love you.
Nicky

April 27, 1943
Nicky Darling,

The weather here has been so good that we can sit on the porch, and sleep with the windows wide open at night.

Last night I listened to a play, "Soldiers in High Boots" on "Cavalcade of America." The play was about paratroopers in Africa. An officer from Washington said that the paratroopers fought with distinction. He said a place in North Carolina will be named Camp Mackall in memory of the first paratrooper killed in action in Africa.

When I get big, I'm going to stay at Pearl's. I'll be closer to the doctor and the hospital. Pearl's neighbors mind their own business. They don't visit every day and sit talking for hours like our kin folks do. I don't want every aunt and cousin in Irondale asking me a hundred questions about you and the baby.

James is in Billings General Hospital in Fort Benjamin Harrison, Indiana. He'll have a final check up, and then he'll come home.

You're right; I should go to church. Even though I don't go, I try to live right. Maybe I'll go to church with you.

Honey, do you need money to get to Alabama? Do you want to stay at the Redmont Hotel? We could do that, or we might be able to get a small, furnished apartment near Five Points for a couple of weeks. It would cost about seven dollars a week. Then I could cook for you. We could be alone and pretend we were civilians.

Love always,

Opal and Nicky Jr.

April 28, 1943

Dearest Opal,

If everything goes well, I should see you in a few days. I'm trying to get an 11-day furlough. When I get to Birmingham, we will do anything you want to do, go out for a drink, to eat, go to the movies.

I couldn't write last night because we had a blackout. Yesterday the whole company went swimming. I did some diving and had a long swim. Did you know that your husband is a good swimmer? Can a woman in your condition go swimming?

I love you so much. I don't know what I'll do when I go across. I will have your picture and your love, and I will know that you and Junior are waiting for me. Lights out. I'll see you soon.

I Love You,

Nicky

April 30, 1943

Nicky Darling,

Dad went to the Post Office this morning to mail my letter, and I hated to ask him to go again this afternoon. I thought I'd wait until tomorrow, but I was afraid I wouldn't sleep. I'd just lie awake thinking about that letter waiting for me. About 4:45 P.M. I took off, and I got to the P.O. just in time. Now that I've read your letter, I'll sleep like a baby, and I hope I'll dream of you. The letters you mail in the morning get here in less than three days.

A couple of cousins came to visit yesterday. They tell everything they hear, so I didn't say anything about Nicky Junior. They kept saying how good I looked, and I kept holding my stomach in. Everyone will know soon enough.

Say Hon, don't make the Captain mad. He might not let you come home. That d— guy. He doesn't know a good soldier when he sees one. After your furlough, tell him to go to h—.

Love you,

Opal

May 1943

At the Trident Conferences, Roosevelt and Churchill agreed to provide American air forces and ground forces to fight in the China-Burma-India (C.B.I.) Theater of Operations. C. B. I. was called the "forgotten war" because so few resources were put into it.

As American forces liberated islands in the Aleutians, Axis troops in North Africa resisted American advances. On May 12, Axis forces in North Africa surrendered.

Allies continued bombing Italy and in Britain, Americans built their first airfield for the 8th Air Force. R.A.F. bombers destroyed hydroelectric plants in Germany.

★★★★★★★★★★★★★

May 1, 1943
Dear Opal,

I worked all day yesterday. In the evening, as I was getting ready to write to you, we went out to fight a forest fire. We didn't get back until 2:00 A.M.

I will not come to Birmingham on Wednesday, but I will be down before Sunday May 9. The company clerk told me that I am supposed to leave Saturday May 8, so I may be there by noon on Sunday. I'll fly down if I can. I'll send a telegram to let you know when I'll arrive. If I don't get a furlough, I'm going to take a few days on my own hook. What do you think of that? I'm proud to be a paratrooper, and I want to fight for my country, but sometimes I hate the army. When you get my telegram, you can look for a place for us to stay. You know, I'd like to see a baseball game while I'm in Birmingham.

I'm listening to "Me and My Gal" on The Hit Parade. I've heard Frank Sinatra sing "That Old Black Magic." Number 5 on the Hit Parade is "You'd Be So Nice to Come Home To."

Soon we will have been married six months, and I love you just as much as I did the day we got married. In fact, I love you more.

Always yours,
Nicky

May 2, 1943
My Darling Wife,

Today is Sunday, and even though I went to 9:00 A.M. Mass, I feel blue. I counted on being with you. We ate a good dinner, and then we put on our old clothes and played baseball until suppertime. We had hash for supper, and it was terrible. Tomorrow we're going into the field, and we won't be back until Wednesday. I can hardly wait to see you.

Forever Yours,
Nicky

May 3, 1943
Nicky Darling,

You wouldn't take a few days off without permission, would you? I'm afraid you might get into trouble if you did that. Have you thought about what you want to do after the war? We will have to make the best of army life until then. You are doing your part, and I am proud of you. We had two blackouts this week, and I thought of you.

Sunday May 9 is Mother's Day, and I am a mother. I appreciate my Mom very much. She never has a selfish thought. And she is grateful for the smallest things. If she sees a flower in the yard that she didn't plant, she calls it a "volunteer," and she is pleased to have it. Dad is also very kind.

James is ready to come home and go dancing. I'll bet he won't be doing as much "high stepping" as he thinks. He may be here when you come on furlough. Friday night Tony Pastor is bringing a big floorshow to the Municipal auditorium. I wish we could go.

Mom is letting the seams out on some of my clothes so I can continue to wear them. Could I go swimming? The problem would be finding a swimsuit large enough. Last night I felt Nicky Jr. kick for the first time.

Always yours,
Opal and Junior

May 4, 1943
Nicky Darling,

It seems like ten years since I've seen you. I'm sitting in a rocking chair on the front porch, wishing you were here. You know, I was listening to The Hit Parade at the same time you were last Saturday night, and I was thinking of you.
Our cousin Johnny Keith, Uncle Bill's son who is stationed in Gulfport, Mississippi, came by to see us. He's a mess sergeant, and he's proud of his stripes. He's looking forward to meeting you. He knows what fine soldiers the paratroopers are. This afternoon, Aunt Ella and Uncle Jim, Dad's brother, came to visit. I showed them your picture.

When you send the telegram telling me you're coming, send it early. The telegraph office at the depot in Irondale closes at six o'clock, and if I don't get it before then, I won't get it until the next morning.

The Inkspots will be in Birmingham next Tuesday night. We could go to see them, and we could see a baseball game, but cabdrivers are on strike, and travel is inconvenient.

Junior is kicking up a storm tonight.

Love always,
Opal

```
WESTERN UNION

SAMFORD    NCAR    MAY 6

MRS. NICHOLAS BONILLA
1920 3RD AVE SO
IRONDALE ALA

TRAIN ARRIVES 11:20 AM WEDNESDAY TERMINAL STATION.

LOVE   NICKY.
```

★★★★★★★★★★★★★

No letters or other documents indicate whether Nicky got a furlough or whether he took "a few days on his own hook." Even if he had a furlough, Nicky may have returned to Fort Bragg late, because, once again, he was "busted." Subsequent letters were addressed to Pfc. Nicholas L. Bonilla, B Company.

Chapter Four

The Tennessee Maneuvers

JUNE 1943

As the Allies waged war in the Mediterranean, *Il Duche*, Fascist Prime Minister Benito Mussolini warned Italians of the threat of invasion.

The R.A.F. struck radar factories in Germany and Italy. The 8th Air Force bombed shipyards where German submarines, *Unterseeboots*, were built, and they bombed Düsseldorf, Munster, and Cologne.

At Fort Bragg, men of the 101st trained for the worst conditions of war. They ran until they dropped; they went days without sleep; they ate K-rations, often canned meat and beans, and used only equipment that could be delivered by parachute, glider, or transport aircraft. Troopers had to march twenty-five miles in eight hours, five miles in one hour, and nine miles in two hours, with full equipment. Those who could not meet the criteria washed out of airborne units. Troopers ran obstacle courses, trained for night fighting, and fought in simulated city streets with targets appearing suddenly and with live ammunition exploding around them.

For maneuvers, the 101st went to Springfield, Tennessee. Regiments were stationed at Camp Campbell, Kentucky, and Evansville, Indiana. Troopers established roadblocks, captured bridges, and cut communications. Glider forces proved their effectiveness. At the end of the

In Camp during the Tennessee Maneuvers
National Archives

maneuvers, the 101st was a battle-ready team. On June 10, the 506th under the command of Col. Robert F Sink was attached to the 101st

★★★★★★★★★★★★★

June 7, 1943
Dear Opal,

Just a line to let you know that I arrived in Evansville, Indiana, this morning. The weather is good and we're setting up camp. The train ride was not bad. We went south to Atlanta where we stayed from noon until 2:00 P.M.; then we came north to Evansville.

I am writing this note on stolen time, so I can't write much. I love you and miss you, and I hope we'll be together soon. Take care of yourself.

Lots of love,
Nicky

June 21, 1943
Opal Sweetheart,

I'm sorry I kept you waiting for a letter. I couldn't write while I was in Tennessee. I wrote Monday June 7, and Tuesday June 8, we went to the Evansville airport, got on planes, and jumped into Tennessee. We were in Tennessee until yesterday. I received only three letters from you, and I was a little disappointed. You said you were going to write to me every day.

I'm so sorry I missed seeing you in Atlanta. I'm glad you got home safe. I thought you might be there, and I looked for you on the platform, but I didn't see you. There were hundreds of people at the station, and I couldn't get off the train. I wish we had met, if only for an hour or two. You say you arrived in Atlanta at 9:00 A.M. and did not get a train until 5:45 P.M. That was a long wait. I knew there was only a chance that we would meet.

Dr. Scott said he would take care of everything for you and Junior for $150. Does he want it all at once, or can we pay monthly? Remember, you are supposed to get six more bonds and an insurance policy.

The food you sent me and Angelini lasted well. The cheese was excellent. The wax melted off the paper, but that was O. K. Angelini said to tell you thanks for being so swell to him. I love you.

Always yours,
Nicky

June 21, 1943
My Darling,

I'm writing again by candlelight. (I need a few more good heavy candles.) The last time I wrote by candlelight, I was wearing gloves, overcoat, boots, and a hat. Now I'm lying in my shorts in the same tent but with both ends open.

How are you, Junior, and all the family? Last night I went to Evansville to take a bath and eat. Evansville is a war town with two airplane factories and two ammunition factories. Restaurants and cocktail lounges are nice, and the people treat us soldiers well. We are the first parachute troops they've seen.

I went to a stage show featuring Lawrence Welk and his Champagne Music. After the show, I went to a bar called the Oasis and drank a nightcap. I know you would like it here.

Yours always,
Nicky

June 25, 1943
Dear Opal,

Sorry I skipped a few days writing, but Wednesday we made another jump in Tennessee, and we didn't get back until noon today. I'm in Evansville. It is hot, much hotter than it was in Alabama. I'm sitting in the shade, but sweat is pouring off me. It'll cool off when the sun goes down. Then the crickets will be as loud as New York taxicabs.

I'm hearing rumors. Some of the boys say we'll stay on maneuvers for a few more weeks; then we'll go back to Fort Bragg, get new equipment, and go across. So far, they are just rumors; don't worry.

Angelini came into the tent and asked me if I was writing to you, and he said to tell you hello. We've been sharing a tent since we went on maneuvers. Angelini is a little lazy, but otherwise, he's a good buddy.

I am lucky to have a dear wife and to be expecting a sweet baby.
Nicky

June 26, 1943
Opal Sweetheart,

Are you worried about me? Please forgive me. Sometimes it's impossible to write.

Today is Saturday and after breakfast, we did calisthenics and then swam for the rest of the morning. I received two letters dated June 22 and 23. You say you can't write when you're worried. Darling, when I go oversees, you will have to write no matter how worried you are, or you will break my heart. No, Darling, you have not been acting like a two-year old child. It is natural for you to worry. When I go across, I'll find some way to let you know.

Is Mom having a good time visiting her brothers in Tennessee? I know you miss her. Say Hon, do we still owe Dad that fifty dollars, or have you been able to pay him back?

Hope to see you soon,
Nicky

June 28, 1943
Opal Sweetheart,

You asked me if we are staying at a new camp. No, we're 40 miles from the nearest camp. We're staying in an open field in the country.

Today I drove some sick boys to the hospital in Camp Breckenridge [Kentucky] about 45 miles from here. The camp has about 35,000 American soldiers and 9,000 German prisoners of war captured in Africa. So, I went to see what the Master Race looks like. I was surprised; those prisoners are the youngest soldiers I've ever seen. Not one seemed to be more than 20 years old. They looked puny to me. I wouldn't trade one of our soldiers for ten of theirs. That's how superior our soldiers are.

[German prisoners of war were held at Camp Campbell and Fort Knox, Kentucky. In Alabama, POWs were held in Camp Aliceville, Camp Opelika, Camp Rucker, Camp Sibert, and Fort McClellan. During the war, the U.S. interned nearly 426,000 Axis soldiers in approximately 700 camps.]

Do I miss you? Did Romeo miss Juliet? Did Napoleon miss Josephine? Would the United States miss Roosevelt?

I love you,
Nicky

June 29, 1943
Dear Opal,

About this time last year, we met. Do you remember? I do. I remember everything about Birmingham, Romeo's, and you . . . .

The weather here has been hot and sticky. It rains almost every day, not for long, only for an hour or two. . . .

Yours always,
Nicky

July 1943

Allied troops liberated North Africa, and strategists decided that an attack on Sicily would secure shipping lanes in the Mediterranean, divert troops from the Russian front, and intensify pressure on Italy. Meanwhile, men and war materiel would be sent to England in preparation for the cross-channel attack.

Churchill and Roosevelt issued a joint appeal for the surrender of Italy. Italians, they said, must decide if they would die for Mussolini and Hitler or live for Italy and civilization.

While the 101st was on maneuvers, the 82nd Airborne Division prepared to invade Sicily in Operation Husky. On July 10, the 3,400 men of the 82nd jumped in darkness and high winds. They were badly scattered, but they offered enough resistance to buy time for Allied ground forces. They occupied Palermo and Trepan, but the 82nd paid a great price for these successes. On July 11, twenty-three C-47s carrying troopers of the 504th Parachute Infantry Regiment were hit by Allied (friendly) fire. Three hundred men were killed. The operation ended August 17 when American troops took Messina.

★ ★ ★ ★ ★ ★ ★ ★ ★ ★ ★ ★ ★

July 8, 1943
Darling Opal,

I am lying in my tent on the top of a mountain, and I am writing to my loving wife. I'm using one of the candles you sent me. I'm sorry you had to wait so long for a letter, but after I wrote the last letter, we packed up to leave.

We got on trucks in Evansville and rode all the way to Tennessee, about 30 miles from Nashville. As soon as we hit Tennessee, we met the "enemy" and from that day, we were always on the go. I didn't take my boots off for five days, and I haven't shaved since we left Evansville, so you can imagine how filthy I feel. Remember the chigger bites I got on the Carolina Maneuvers? They were nothing compared to what I have now. I have bites from head to toe. All the other boys are in the same shape. We will be here until Sunday or Monday when we go on the next phase of maneuvers.

We've been fighting a "war" day and night, catching up on our sleep when we can. We came into camp today, and we were all tired and hungry, but before we did anything else, we asked for our mail. I got the most mail in the company—nine letters from you, two packages, and three letters from New York. As soon as I took my pack off, I read your letters.

And Darling, thanks for my cake. The icing was superb and the coconut was excellent. I ate almost half of it before I knew what I was doing. I gave Angelini a piece, and he said it was the best he'd ever tasted. About a quarter of it is left. Tell Fred thanks for the candles. They last a long time.

Is Nicky Jr. bothering you? I am glad Dr. Scott says you and the baby are healthy. I can hardly wait for the day when I'll take you in my arms again.

Love always,
Nicky

July 9, 1943
My Dearest Opal,

We didn't work today. We cleaned our rifles and equipment and shined our shoes. Some of the boys washed clothes, but I didn't have to. I brought plenty from camp.

Please send more candles when you get a chance. I have only two left because I've given as many as I can spare to the boys. They are a good bunch of boys, but they don't always plan like they should.

Tonight we drove a Jeep to a store and bought ten pounds of potatoes, four dozen eggs, and two pounds of butter, four loaves of bread, tomato juice, and sugar. We came back to camp, started a fire, fried potatoes and eggs, and made coffee. I was the chef, and some of the boys called me "Nick of the Waldorf." Not a crumb was left. Someday I'd like to take you on a picnic and cook for you like I cooked for the boys.

Darling, I lost my wallet, and now I don't have a picture of you. Please send one as soon as possible.

Always yours,
Nicky

July 10, 1943
Hello Darling,

The mountains are every shade of green and blue imaginable. When the sun sets, the sky turns purple and a breeze begins to blow. Angelini and I pitched our tent under a cedar tree. We're cool all day, and we sleep under blankets at night. I haven't been to Nashville or any of the other towns close by. I do not care to go anywhere without you. Angelini received a package of food and I'm helping him eat it—sausage, Spam, crackers, jelly and candy. I got a letter from you, and as always, I was glad.

Tomorrow morning we begin a new maneuver. We're working hard, but I dread going back to Fort Bragg—that is just one step closer to going across.

Did you show Dad, James, and Fred my trench knife with the brass knuckles? If they want knives like it, I'll get them.

I'm glad James is working. He'll be busy during the day, and at night, he can go gallivanting. If I were single, I'd be in my glory around all those girls who don't have boyfriends, but I'm a happily married man.

Always yours,
Nicky

July 12, 1943
Darling Opal,

Early yesterday morning we started walking with full packs and walked until 6:00 P.M. Then we dug foxholes and trenches, went back about a mile, and ate supper. We're defending a big hill. I won't be able to mail letters for a while, but I'll write a little every chance I get.

I've been thinking about Junior. He will have a bright future. He might grow up to be President of the United States. What do you think?

3:00 P.M.

I just finished dinner—ham, carrots, potatoes, bread and butter. Only water to drink, but I got my stove and my sterno and made a cup of powdered coffee. All the soldiers around me are asleep. Only the guard and I are still awake, and I'm drifting off, thinking of you.

5:00 P.M.

I slept a while, and now a cool wind is blowing. The "enemy" is close. I can hear them shouting, maybe 3 miles away. They'll be on top of us soon, so I have to go.

7:00 P.M.

Hi Toots. I can hardly wait until I get back to base camp so I can get my mail.

July 13
7:00 A.M.

The enemy raided us last night and captured our kitchen. I'm hungry, and I don't have anything to eat in my pack. I haven't been able to shave, so I have a big beard. I'll be glad when I can get a shave, a bath, and some clean clothes. An airplane just flew over and dropped a sack of flour—it was supposed to be a bomb.

11:00 A.M.

Still no breakfast. The enemy is on top of us, and the company commander said to get everything ready to move.

July 14

When we moved out yesterday, the enemy was hot on our trail. They chased us until midnight, and all that time, we had nothing to eat or drink, not even water. We were exhausted. We lay down and slept until 6:00 A.M., when we got up, and breakfast was waiting for us.

We attacked a bridge and we fought all day. We took it, and we left a few men on guard. Then we went to a high hill and rested. The enemy attacked a town about three miles away, and we went to defend it. We drove the enemy out; now we're ready to sleep. We've been fighting around these towns: Hartsville, Bellwood, Lebanon, Carthage, Nashville, and McMinnville. Are these towns near the town in Tennessee where Mom grew up? [As a child and as a young woman, Louise Keith lived in Pleasant Hill, Tennessee, near Copperhill.]

July 15

Good morning, Darling. Slept well and ate hard-boiled eggs, bacon, and sliced peaches for breakfast. As we were eating, an airplane flew over and sounded a siren. The war is over (and I wish it was).

We've packed up and we're waiting for trucks to take us to an airport so we can fly to Fort Bragg or some other place.

I love you,
Nicky

July 15, 1943
Dearest,

Here I am Darling, waiting for supper, and I'm very hungry. We're going to eat, wash, shave, shine our shoes, and board trucks to return to Evansville. I'll write more later.

I love you,
Nicky

July 16, 1943
Hello, Darling,

Last night about 7:00, we got on trucks and rode all night, a trip of about 175 miles. There were 22 men on each truck, so we had to sit up all the way. We couldn't sleep.

We got back to Evansville about 8:00 A.M. We pitched our tents and then ate breakfast. We are going back to Fort Bragg Sunday or Monday.

Yours always,
Nicky

July 19, 1943
Dearest Opal,

How are you, Sweet? I'm riding a train to Fort Bragg and should be back at camp tomorrow. I received your package. When I get a package, the boys say, "Your wife certainly loves you." and I say, "I wouldn't take a million dollars for my wife." You know I mean it. Also received your pictures. How sweet and lovely you are. Didn't get the wallet. I'll probably get that at Fort Bragg.

I can hardly wait for our little rascal to be born. I hope I'm in the U.S. when he or she arrives.

Always yours,
Nicky

July 22, 1943
Darling Opal,

I'm back in Fort Bragg, in the same barracks, in the same bed. I'd like to be at home sitting on the porch with you.

I believe we'll be going across in a month. We're getting new equipment and making other preparations. The war seems to be going well. So far, we are winning, and I think we'll have all of Sicily before long. We may jump into Italy after Sicily is taken.

I received the package with the anchovies, caviar, and sardines. I appreciate all that good stuff, but you should save your money. You will need it when the baby comes. One thing I need is Beville's Lotion.

If our Blessed Event wasn't so close, I'd ask you to come up here and spend a few days with me, but making that long tiresome trip wouldn't be good for you.

If the baby is a boy, you can name him. Names for girls I like are Maureen, Sandra, Catherine, Jean, and Joan. Do you like these?

Let's think about how happy we'll be when I come home. I know you do not go to church much, but when I leave, please go and pray for my safe return.

This is the first good night's sleep I will have since we left Evansville, and I hope I dream of you. Pat Nicky Jr. and tell him his dad is asking for him.

Forever yours,

Nicky

July 24, 1943

Dear Opal,

We've been working hard, but it feels good to sleep in a bed and to eat regular food. Haven't been to Fayetteville. Tonight I went to the movie in camp and saw Bing Crosby and Dorothy Lamour in "Dixie," a picture about the beginning of minstrel shows.

I received the wallet. It's just the kind I wanted, and I put two pictures of you in it.

I'm trying hard to get a furlough, but don't know if I will. Not much time before lights out, so I'll say goodnight. I know we will always love each other as much as we do now.

You always,

Nicky

July 30, 1943

Dearest Opal,

The time draws near when I will leave the U.S.A., and God only knows when I will be coming back. Last week we flew to New York to load a ship with equipment and supplies. We slept on the ship. I wanted to visit my family, but the company commander said our arrival was secret. If we tried to communicate with anybody in the city, we would be considered spies. Most of the boys did not know where we were.

I'm back at Fort Bragg, and I probably shouldn't be writing this. Our mail is being censored. We are not allowed to go to town, and no one is allowed to visit us.

Say Darling, how about sending me another cake. It may be the last one I'll get in the U.S.A. I believe my wife is the best cook south of the Mason Dixon line. Send me a list with all family birthdays, and I will try to send cards. Tell Farris I'll bring him a Jap for a pet.

I Love You.

Nicky

AUGUST 1943

Operation Husky ended when General Patton's troops took Messina. The entire operation lasted only thirty-nine days. U.S. planes attacked Naples, and the R.A.F. bombed Milan. Benito Mussolini was imprisoned, and the Allies demanded the unconditional surrender of Italy. The Italian government declared Rome an "Open City." Despite continued German resistance, the Italian government would offer no opposition to Allies entering the city. Because of Allied successes in Italy, the German government evacuated one million women, children, elderly, and infirm from Berlin.

At the Quebec Conference, Roosevelt and Churchill approved plans for a cross-channel invasion of France.

★★★★★★★★★★★★★

August 5, 1943
Darling Opal,

I haven't received a letter from you in a week, and I'm worried, but maybe the censors are taking their time. I'm enclosing a clipping about maternity benefits for soldiers' wives. Ask Dr. Scott about it.

How are you, my sweet? Is everything all right with you? I'm very blue. I'll go across soon, and I don't know when I'll see you again. I do know that I have a fine girl waiting for me. When I return, I will only love you more.

I might come to Birmingham. I've asked the big shots to let me have a few days off, and they are thinking about it. [This vague statement suggests that Nicky was planning to go A.W.O.L.]

Love always,
Nicky

★★★★★★★★★★★★★

An article from the *Birmingham News* reveals the difficulties soldiers and their wives experienced in getting dependent medical care for dependents:

> MATERNITY FUND NOW AVAILABLE: MONEY WILL BE USED TO CARE FOR WIVES, BABIES OF SERVICE MEN
>
> Alabama has received additional Federal funds to finance free maternity and pediatric care for the wives and babies of service men and this program is now being resumed after suspension in January.
>
> The small sum formerly available was exhausted at that time, but health officials now believe it can be continued for the duration and at least six months thereafter . . . .
>
> Physicians and hospitals participating in the program are paid by the

> Government through the health department. Hospital beds are so much in demand, however, that they cannot always be made available to *[the maternity]* patient.
>
> Participation by physicians and hospitals is voluntary . . . and some physicians are declining to take part in the belief that such a program is a definite step toward socialized medicine, strongly opposed generally by private practitioners.

Despite the statement above, Opal did not receive authorization for hospital care for the birth of her baby. A statement from the Alabama State Health Department, Bureau of Maternal and Child Care reads as follows: " Medical care for confinement at home only effective from September 10, 1943. There are no participating hospitals in Birmingham, and hospital care cannot be authorized or paid for." Nicky and Opal paid for Opal's hospitalization from their own pockets.

★★★★★★★★★★★★★

August 6, 1943
Opal, My Sweet,

How are you and how is Nicky Jr.? Is that little bugger giving you any trouble? Hey You! Don't say you don't want the baby to look like you. If we have a girl, I hope she looks just like you. Here are a couple more articles for the scrapbook. When I come home, we'll look at it together.

Love always,
Nicky

★★★★★★★★★★★★★

Nicky got a few days leave, or he went "over the hill." He visited Opal in Birmingham, and he returned to her the letters she had written to him. When Nicky was shipped overseas, letters would be more strictly censored, and soldiers would not be able to keep letters from home.

An article in *Good Housekeeping*, November 1942, advised readers about the censors' rules:

> Don't identify by name or location factories or facilities engaged in war work. In particular, don't describe new plants. Don't tell where a war factory is shipping its products . . . . Don't describe new products.
>
> Don't identify the country where your soldier is stationed. That's why you address mail for overseas delivery to an Army Post Office (A.P.O. number) in the United States. Don't inquire about the Scottish landscape or the Egyptian climate. Don't identify the unit or branch of service of friends.

> Don't write detailed accounts of weather over here . . . . Last year, hundreds of letters were held up while the censors deleted accounts of towns isolated and power plants put out of commission by a storm in the South.
>
> Don't repeat rumors and "inside stories." Don't be abusive about the government, the army, or our Allies.[6]

From April 1943 through September 1944, only Nicky's letters were saved. One letter from Opal to Nicky was returned, and it is transcribed here.

★ ★ ★ ★ ★ ★ ★ ★ ★ ★ ★ ★ ★

August 19, 1943
Opal Darling,

When I left you at the train station in Birmingham, I was afraid you would cry, so I'm glad you left quick. I always knew that you would be brave. I am very proud of you. I was crying inside, wondering when I would ever see you again.

It was wonderful to be with you, to see you, touch you, kiss you. Your family treated me like one of their own. I enjoyed the meals at Mom's, but I'll let you in on a secret. I like the cakes you cook better than Mom's. Now listen here, young lady, don't tell Mom. It might hurt her feelings, and I don't want to do that.

My trip to Fayetteville was not bad. The train wasn't too crowded, and I rode in an air-conditioned car.

I will not be in the U.S.A. when Nicky Jr. is born, but my heart and soul will be with you, then and always.

Nicky

August 21, 1943
My Darling Wife,

The news we have been waiting for has come. Please, for your sake, and for the baby's, don't worry. I'll write as soon as possible, but keep writing to me at the same address, and my mail will be forwarded.

As I write, I am remembering when we first met. When I saw you, I thought heaven was missing an angel. I asked you for a date, and you said no because you were going to a party. Then I asked you for a date for the next Saturday and you said yes. I came by Romeo's and you had almost forgotten our date. After you finished work, we played miniature golf; then we went for a nightcap. That night I knew I was in love with you, but you weren't sure.

I will never forget the night I came back from New York. I took you to dinner at Tom's Steak House, and you said you were hungry, but you didn't eat a bite. You just looked at me. Then I knew that you loved me as I loved you. The next time I came to Birmingham, you met me at the train, and you were blushing.

Do you remember the night before we were married? I said terrible things to you, but you didn't say a word. I wanted you to despise me so much that you wouldn't marry me. I was afraid that marrying me, a soldier, might ruin your life. And then you loved me enough to forgive me and marry me. I thank God for that. Our wedding ceremony was simple but sacred, and I'll always remember it. I will love, honor, and cherish you for the rest of my life, just as I vowed.

Remember when you knew you were going to have a baby? You were upset, afraid that you might not be a good mother. Well, the little bugger will be here in a few weeks, and you and I will the happiest parents in the world. Send me a picture of you and the baby as soon as you can. If it's a girl, name her Sandra Maureen.

Darling, until you hear from me, be brave and true, and when I return, I will be the best husband I can be. I love you dearly,

Nicky

Camp Shanks, New York

The Fort Bragg post band played on August 22, 1943, as Nicky and other soldiers of the 101st boarded trains bound for Camp Shanks in suburban New York. Lying beside the Hudson River, Camp Shanks was the last stop in the United States for more than 1.3 million soldiers who departed to the European Theatre of Operations. Some 47,000 soldiers lived in barracks 20 feet wide by 100 feet long, with two rows of bunks.

At Shanks, soldiers of the 101st were provided full equipment. No large depots for the storage of equipment were available in England, so the men took essentials with them. When troopers went on alert, they knew they would ship out in twelve hours. The 502nd would be bused to the southern tip of Manhattan Island, to the New York port of embarkation. Nicky was near his old hometown, but he might as well have been thousands of miles away.

Pier 88 in New York. The 101st departed for England from this pier.

★★★★★★★★★★★★★★

August 27, 1943
Opal Darling,

I'll bet you can guess where I am. I'm in a cool climate, so cool that I used two blankets on my bed last night. The food here is good, ten times better than where I was before. I've received forwarded mail and the letter you sent to the new address. I went to personnel yesterday and signed to have the allotment, insurance, and savings bonds sent to your address in Irondale. I told personnel that you are having a baby in two weeks, and they told me that all expenses will be taken care of.

Yours forever,
Nicky

August 30, 1943
My Dearest Opal,

The next letter you get could come from anywhere-Africa, Sicily, Alaska, Norway, or Greece, but no matter how long you have to wait to hear from me, please continue to write, and always remember that no news is good news.

Darling, I am so worried. Nicky Junior will be here in a few weeks, and I'm afraid you won't have enough money. I don't have any money to send you. We have not been paid. The army is afraid that if the boys had train fare, some of them would desert. I swallowed my pride and wrote to my mother asking for money, but I have not heard from her. I don't know which way to turn. As soon as I'm paid, I'll send you all I can.

The First Sergeant just came in and told us to go to the dispensary to get shots.

I love you with all my heart.
Nicky

September 1943

The Italian Government signed an armistice to become effective September 8, but German forces continued to occupy Rome and counterattacked allied forces at Salerno. Nazis freed Mussolini from prison, and accompanied him to Vienna and then to Munich. The people of Naples revolted against the Nazis who had forced Italians to work in war plants. German forces sent tanks against the rebels, but insurgents set fire to eight tanks. Allies reached Naples, and retreating Nazis plundered the art treasures of many Italian cities.

Aboard the H.M.S. Strathnaver and in St. Johns, Newfoundland

Nicky sailed to England aboard *H.M.S. Strathnaver*, a British ship built in 1931; she was designed for 500 first class and 670 tourist class passengers. In 1939, she was refitted as a troop ship with a capacity of 4,300. For this voyage, more than 5,800 men of the 101st and 160 members of the Women's Army Corps were jammed into the ship.

Tugboats pushed the ship through New York Harbor, and soldiers gathered at the rail to take what might be their last look at the Statue of Liberty.

Soldiers wore helmets and life jackets at all times, ate two meals a day, and took salt-water showers. They could go to a canteen during two hours of the day. Soldiers slept in hammocks, "as crowded as a bunch of bananas," according to Robert Bowen, a glider trooper in the 401st.[7] Soldiers observed strict blackouts, and those on poorly-ventilated lower decks came to A deck periodically for fresh air and exercise.

The ship departed in a convoy on September 5. Early on September 6, German submarines torpedoed a destroyer in the convoy, and the crew of the Strathnaver conducted a successful boat drill. However, the concussion of explosions damaged the Strathnaver. Freshwater tanks were taking on salt water. On September 11, the ship put in at St. Johns, Newfoundland. While repairs were made, the harbor town was declared off limits, and troops were required to stay on the ship. Soldiers spent their time reading, writing, gambling, and watching movies set up by the Red Cross in warehouses adjoining the docks.

Troops marched to Fort Pepperell on September 13 and 14. There they washed and cleaned clothes and equipment. They saw movies, went to dances, and visited a temporary beer hall. On September 20, troops marched from Ft. Pepperell back to the ship. The ship was not ready for boarding, so marches continued.

The *Strathnaver* put out to sea on September 26, but she struck rocks and returned to St. Johns for repairs. The ship headed out again on September 27, but she returned because a load shifted and she took on 28 inches of water. Through September 28, 29, and 30, troops again marched in the area of Fort Pepperell.

Troops boarded the *U.S.S. John Ericsson* on October 3. It was no luxury liner, but it was more comfortable than the *Strathnaver*. On October 4, the *Ericsson* sailed for Halifax, Nova Scotia, for refueling and reprovisioning. Late on October 6, the *Ericsson* joined a convoy from the States, and on October 18, the ship docked at Liverpool. Troops had been in transit for 44 days. They were awarded the American Theater Ribbon for their ordeal.

★ ★ ★ ★ ★ ★ ★ ★ ★ ★ ★ ★ ★

September 4, 1943
Hello Darling,

Glad to hear from you. Hope you're feeling good. I'm fine, and I've been well since I left.

Darling, next time you write, use V-mail stationery; I'll get your letters much faster. I can't write much.

Please send me a telegram when Junior arrives.

Pfc. Nicholas L. Bonilla
Asn. 6877454 Co. D
502nd Parachute Infantry
A. P.O. 47
N. Y. C., N. Y.

Love always,
Nicky

[Nicky had transferred from B Company to D Company.]

September 30, 1943 [St. Johns, Newfoundland]
Dear Opal,

This is the first chance I've had to write since I left the states. I know you've been waiting a long time for this letter. Well, you have nothing on me; I've been waiting a long time to write it. I haven't heard from you. I won't get mail until I reach my final destination. We've been delayed. All I can say is that I am not in the U.S.A.

I'm dying to know if I'm the father of a boy or a girl. I hope it won't be long before I see you and the baby. I know the war is not going to last much longer.

I Love You,
Nicky

Chapter Five

Somewhere in England

October 1943

As the Allies began preparations for a cross-channel attack, Allied bombers struck Vienna, Kassel, and Schweinfurt. Sixty attacking aircraft were shot down, and 138 were severely damaged. The government of the U.S.A. granted aid to the U.S.S.R; Money and materiel would be provided until June 1944. In the Moscow Conferences, Allied leaders agreed to accept nothing less than the unconditional surrender of Germany.

Children in ruins in London
National Archives

Men of the 101st rode trains from Liverpool to camps about eighty miles southwest of London. The 502nd was based in the Chilton-Foliat area in Wiltshire, near Stonehenge, and in the Denford and Hungerford areas in Berkshire. Officers lived in English manor houses such as Littlecote House, Denford House, or Basildon Manor. Enlisted men lived in barracks, stables, metal huts, and tents. Soldiers trained constantly in the wet and cold, and food was in short supply.

Nevertheless, American troops ate better rations, wore better uniforms, used better equipment, and earned better pay than their British counterparts. Among themselves, the Tommies [named for Tommy Atkins, the sample name printed on British Army forms] said, "There's nothing wrong with the Yanks, except that they are over-paid, over-sexed, and over here."

The 101st continued training with fifteen to twenty-five mile hikes, close combat drills, chemical warfare exercises, and first aid and map reading instruction. General William C. Lee, commander of the 101st, suffered a heart attack and was replaced by General Maxwell Taylor.

In the U.S., women in the work force made the nation the "arsenal of democracy." More than six million women worked in airplane factories, shipyards, and munitions plants. They drove taxis, streetcars, and tractors. They were clerks, lawyers, and baseball players.

The symbol of America's working women was Rosie the Riveter, an image painted by Norman Rockwell that appeared on the cover of the May 29, *Saturday Evening Post*. Rosie was depicted as a big muscular woman with a cute face and a confident pose. Her rivet gun rested in her lap and the name Rosie was painted on her lunchbox. The women she represented would produce the fighters, bombers, transports, landing ships, and destroyers that would be needed to win the war.

[Undated V-mail letter written between October 15, 1943, and October 21, 1943.]

Dear Opal,

Today is the first time I've heard from you since I left the states. I received your telegram and about twenty letters, and I'm glad to hear that the baby is perfect and you are in good health. About the time Sandra was born, I was crossing the Atlantic Ocean. I went to the Red Cross Representative on the ship to see if I could get news about you and the baby. He told me he would try his best. He said that 35 men on the ship were in the same situation I was in. Dr. Scott's telegram arrived in England about two days after he sent it, but I did not get it until I arrived in England about a month later. Mail was not forwarded to the ship because our location was a military secret.

England is a lush green country. Sheep and cattle graze in pastures separated by stone fences. It reminds me of some places back home, but England or no

England, I want to get back to Alabama to my wife and baby. Are you pleased that the baby is a girl? I know you wanted a boy, but I'm tickled "pink." I won money betting with my buddies that the baby would be a girl.

Send me a picture as soon as you can and a good long letter—ten or twelve pages.

Love always,
Nicky

October 22, 1943
Opal Darling,

I didn't get new mail today, but I don't mind. I'm reading again and again the letters I received yesterday.

The weather here is cold. It has rained every day since I arrived, but we manage to keep dry. We have good barracks, and we keep our raincoats handy.

Today Sandra is exactly one month and 9 days old. Does she look like you? Send me a picture as soon as you can. I want to see our baby, and I want to see if having the baby has changed you.

I Love You,
Nicky

October 23, 1943
Dear Opal,

How is the sweetest mother on earth, and how is our baby? Honey, you have no idea how much I want to see Sandra, even if only in a picture. Now that I'm settled, I'd like you to send that big picture of you that I kept at Fort Bragg.

I wish you and the baby were here with me in England. All the houses are made of stone or brick. Some of them have thatched roofs. Almost every home has a flower garden.

How is your family? How is Patricia? Does she know there is another baby in the house? Tonight I will say a prayer for all of you.

Always yours,
Nicky

October 24, 1943
Hello Darling,

Today is the first day it hasn't rained since I've been in England. It is Sunday, and I got up at 6:00 A.M. and went to 6:30 mass. I said a prayer for you and Sandra, and I know that my prayers will be answered. The church near camp is small. It would hold only about twenty-five people, but it is beautiful. It looks so peaceful that it almost makes me forget the war. I wish you could see it.

Everything in England is rationed, even to soldiers. We are allowed one package of cigarettes a day, one bar of soap a week, and seven pints of beer a week.

That is not nearly enough beer. My buddies and I could drink seven pints of beer in one night. Civilians are wearing suits and dresses with patches. People with automobiles get one gallon of gas a week, and candy bars are a thing of the past.

I haven't been to London yet, but when I go, I want to buy Christmas presents and newspapers. All I want for Christmas is a picture of you and Sandra. There is nothing I would treasure more. I haven't seen a newspaper since I arrived in England, so I have no idea what is going on in the outside world.

I Love You,
Nicky

October 25, 1943
Dear Opal,

Last night I dreamed about us. I dreamed that I was home with you and the baby. We woke up in a pretty bedroom in a nice little house. You cooked a delicious breakfast; then we dressed Sandra, we got dressed, and we went for a walk in the park. The sun was shining, you were smiling, and Sandra in her baby carriage was radiant.

I've been thinking about christening the baby. You know I am a Catholic, but it does not matter to me if you christen the baby as a Catholic or a Protestant. I think your family will be happier if you christen her as a Protestant. As you know, what my family thinks doesn't matter. You do what you think is best.

When are you going to send me a cake? You know I'm crazy about your cakes, and since rationing is so strict, cake is quite a luxury.

Your husband,
Nicky

NOVEMBER 1943

American forces fighting in the Solomon and Gilbert Islands in the Pacific suffered thousands of casualties.

In Europe, Allied bombers attacked airports in Vienna and inflicted heavy damage on Berlin. In occupied France, food was rationed, and fuel was in short supply. Bicycles became the primary means of transportation.

The Allies formed the United Relief and Rehabilitation Administration to assist people hit hardest by the war.

★ ★ ★ ★ ★ ★ ★ ★ ★ ★ ★ ★ ★

November 6, 1943
Dear Opal,

I haven't written because I've been in the field and didn't return until November 5. That day, I was offered a 48-hour pass, and I took it, but I had only a half-hour to get ready. I took the nine letters I received from you and read them on the train.

While we were in the field and walking through the forests, we saw pheasants and rabbits everywhere. We almost stepped on them. Some of the boys wanted to bag a few birds, but we've been ordered not to harm the wildlife.

I was thinking how much I would like to walk down those country roads with you and the baby. You'd wear one of my favorite dresses. I'd be wearing civilian clothes, and the baby, looking like a little doll, would walk or ride in a carriage between us. We'll spend a lot of time outdoors when I come home.

On my pass, I rode the train to a seaside resort. Usually the Red Cross has sleeping facilities for soldiers, but they were full, so I got a room in a hotel. I stayed there two days, ate all my meals there, and it cost me only one pound and two shillings, or $4.40.

I looked for Christmas presents, and I saw some things I wanted to buy, but you must have ration points to buy anything except liquor, beer, and food in restaurants. So I'll send money, and you can buy gifts for yourself, Sandra, and the family.

The saloons here are called pubs, and barmaids serve the drinks. The beer is putrid—warm and flat. I can't drink more than one or two. The Scotch tastes good, but the amount each pub can sell is limited, so it's first come, first served.

Blackouts are absolute. You could stand in the street in front of a pub or theater and never know it was there.

I love you,
Nicky

November 9, 1943
Dear Opal,

When I see you again, I will fall in love with you just like I did the first time. You'll be my sweetheart once more and forever. . . .

My thoughts are always with you and Sandra.

Love,
Nicky

WESTERN UNION

CK38 CABLE PC NY AMPYRI
VIA COMMERCIAL 8

MRS. NICK BONILLA
IRONDALE ALABAMA

DARLING, I WILL NEVER FORGET NOVEMBER 10. THAT DAY WILL LIVE IN MY HEART ALWAYS. HOPE TO BE WITH YOU BEFORE NEXT ANNIVERSARY.
ALWAYS YOURS,
NICKY
8:15 A M

November 10, 1943
Dearest Opal,

One year ago today, we were married, and that was the happiest day of my life. Did you get the telegram I sent? I went to a movie tonight, and before the picture started, they played "White Christmas." I thought about Christmas last year when we were together. That was another happy day.

Tonight I'm going to say a special prayer asking God to protect a devoted mother and her dear child.

Love always,
Nicky

November 11, 1943
Dearest Opal,

Tomorrow we go into the field until Saturday, so you won't hear from me for a few days. Thank you for the toilet kit. I needed it, especially the razor blades. Razor blades are rationed. We get only two a week, double-edged blades, and I prefer single edged blades. Tell Sandra that the soap she sent was a nice surprise. I need a cigarette lighter. A good one shouldn't be too expensive. Ask James what kind to get. He will know just what a soldier needs.

Darling, you say you weigh 141 pounds. That's a little heavy isn't it, but I know you'll get back to 123 pounds soon.

When mail came today, everyone in my hutment received at least one package. We got plenty of food—fruitcake, olives, popcorn, salami, sardines, anchovies, cashews, and cookies.

Today is Armistice Day, and I am thinking about the boys who fought in World War I. We owe them a lot, and it's a crying shame we have to fight another war. I hope it will soon be over, and I'll come home to you and Sandra.

I Love You,
Nicky

November 12, 1943
Dearest,

I received two letters from you today and a fruitcake! The cake is excellent. Did you make it yourself? When I get home, I want you to make me a fruitcake at least once a week. That's how much I like it. I wish I could be with you and the family for Thanksgiving. Next year I will be there.

Yours always,
Nicky

November 14, 1943
Good evening, Sweetheart,

I wish I could see Sandra. I can imagine holding her in my arms and tossing her up high in the air. I can hear her laughing, and I can feel her wiggling and kicking . . . .

Love forever,
Nicky

November 15, 1943
Hello Dearest,

You probably won't hear from me until Saturday. We're going into the field, and you know it's almost impossible to write then.

Please send me some handkerchiefs. I have only a few, and I can't buy them here because of rationing.

I know you're pleased to have a little girl, but do you still want a boy? Maybe we can do something about that when I get home . . . .

Love always,
Nicky

December 1943

At the Teheran Conference on December 1, Franklin D. Roosevelt, Winston Churchill, and Joseph Stalin agreed that the Allies would invade France from England in 1944 as the U.S.S.R. launched a new offensive from the east. The Allies also agreed that cities liberated by Russian troops would remain under the Soviet sphere of influence. For the first time, Russia was recognized as a world power.

General Eisenhower was appointed Commander-in-Chief of the Allied forces in Europe. General Montgomery was appointed commander of the British 21st Army Group.

Military historian John Keegan described the build-up of American troops in England that he had seen when he was a child:

> Towards the end of 1943, our backwater . . . overflowed almost overnight with G.I.s. How different they looked from our own jumble-sale champions, beautifully clothed in smooth khaki, as fine in cut and quality as a British officer's . . . . [They were] armed with glistening modern automatic weapons, Thompson sub-machine guns, Winchester carbines, Garand self-loading rifles. More striking still were the number, size, and elegance of the vehicles in which they paraded around the countryside in stately convoy . . . . The Americans traveled in magnificent, gleaming olive-green, pressed steel, four-wheel-drive juggernauts . . . decked with deep-tread spare tyres, [sic] winches, towing cables, fire extinguishers.

> There were towering G.M.C. six-by-sixes, compact and powerful Dodge four-by-fours and . . . buzzing nimbly about the lanes . . . tiny and entrancing jeeps . . . . Standing one day at the roadside, . . . I was assaulted from the back of each truck by a volley of small missiles, which fell into the ditch beside me. When I burrowed in the dead leaves to discover the cause, I unearthed . . . a little treasure of Hershey Bars, Chelsea candy, and Jack Frost sugar-cubes, a week's, perhaps a month's ration . . . . There was, I reflected as I crammed the spoil into my pockets, something going on in the west of England about which Adolph Hitler should be very worried indeed.[8]

The invasion could not come soon enough for the people of Holland and France. The Gestapo had expelled 150,000 Dutch Jews from Holland, and the Vichy government in France had arrested 20,000 "terrorists," residents who supported the Allies.

★ ★ ★ ★ ★ ★ ★ ★ ★ ★ ★ ★ ★

December 1, 1943
Opal Darling,

I haven't written in two weeks. Please forgive me. When I went to the field, I had a cold. We were in the field for a week, and it was the coldest week I have ever spent anywhere. It rained constantly. We walked all night. We rested and cooked our food during the day. It was awful. I felt like quitting, but you know how stubborn I am. I stuck it out. When I got back to camp, I was so sick I could hardly walk.

I went to the dispensary, and then I was sent to the hospital. I had the flu, but I've been resting and eating well. I couldn't write from the hospital because our mail must go through the company censor. I'm sorry you had to wait so long for a letter.

I love you,
Nicky

December 2, 1943
Hello Opal Sweetheart,

How are my girls? Today I got thirteen V-Mail letters, two regular letters, and a package. I opened the regular letters first, and saw the pictures of you and Sandra. Sandra is adorable. Seeing your pictures was the beginning of a New World. Married life and motherhood must agree with you, because you are more beautiful than ever.

And Darling, I got another fruitcake. If the first one I got was only half a cake, the whole thing must have been huge.

A proud husband and father,
Nicky

Opal, wearing her wings, and Sandra

December 3, 1943
Dearest Opal,

It seems like ages since I saw you, and it feels like years since I held you in my arms. I want to kiss you until you beg for mercy.

I'm listening to the radio playing one of my favorite tunes, "Sunday, Monday, or Always." I wonder how I got along before I knew you. I couldn't miss you until I knew you, but it seems that I saw you in my dreams before we ever met. So you see, my Darling, I have loved you for a long time.

You know, I think Sandra does look a little like me. She has your mouth, your eyes, and your smile. I'm crossing my fingers that I'll be home soon.

Our barracks looks like the League of Nations. We have two Irish boys, a Scotsman, and two Genuine Rebels, one from Georgia, and one from North Carolina. We have two Poles, a Frenchman, a Russian, two Jews, two Englishmen, a boy from Holland, a Mexican, a German, and of course me, an Italian. But Darling, we are all Americans. Each one is willing to die for the others. We are like one big family.

You asked me if we have a radio. We bought one as soon as we arrived. Radios are expensive; they cost from 15 to 50 pounds. A pound is equivalent to 4 dollars, and there is no note equivalent to a one-dollar bill. Change from a pound is in coins. A half crown is 50 cents, a shilling is 20 cents, a sixpence is 10 cents, a three pence is a nickel, a halfpenny is worth two cents, and a farthing is 1/4 of a cent. Now when you come to England, you'll know just how the money system works.

Give Sandra a big kiss for me.
Nicky

December 15, 1943
Dear Opal,

How are you today? I'm just dandy. I received three packages. Pearl sent me toiletries and two cartons of cigarettes, and James and Fred sent me cigarettes.

They are generous boys, and I know you are proud of them. I received a letter from Dot and a card from Pearl. My in-laws are tops.

I sent you and the baby a cablegram money order for $200 on November 8, and then I sent another for $100 about two weeks later. I sent them through the army. Those cables might take a long time to get to you, so I'm sending a postal money order for another $100.

As I told you, I show Sandra's picture to everyone I see, and some of the boys say she looks like me, and some say she looks like you. What do you think? That photographer must know his business because he caught Sandra in mighty cute poses.

You ask if I need anything. All I need is a lighter, handkerchiefs, and razor-blades.

Next Christmas, I'll take you shopping in New York. We'll go to Macy's, and we'll see the Rockettes at Radio City Music Hall. We'll see the lights at Rockefeller Center, and on Christmas Eve, we'll go to Mass at St. Patrick's.

Love always,
Nicky

December 16, 1943
Dearest Opal,

You asked me to look up Roger Gray [a paratrooper in HQ Company who was married to a woman living in Irondale], and I'll try. His camp is about five miles from here.

There is nothing I like to do more than write to my wife and daughter. I look at your pictures at least three times a day. I show them to the boys that I think so well of. They kid me and say that the baby isn't mine because she is too pretty to

Christmas card and V-mail sent from Nicky to Opal

have an ugly father like me. I say, "That's all right. You see how pretty she is? Can you imagine how gorgeous she'd be if I were good looking?" Then they are as quiet as church mice.

Would you believe it, I'm not allowed to keep your letters more than a week. After I've read them many times, I burn them. I hate to do it, but I have to. Every new letter is a treasure. *[Censors feared that letters from home might unwittingly give information about troop strength and movements.]*

Did you have a nice Thanksgiving dinner? You probably won't get this letter before Christmas. I know you will have a good dinner, and I wish I could be there to enjoy it with you and the family. For Thanksgiving dinner, I had baloney, and then only two slices. With all the "baloney" in the army, you'd think we could have all we want. Christmas dinner will have to be better.

Darling, some of the letters I write to you must get lost because of the war. Ships and planes carry mail, and as you know, enemy submarines sink those ships and enemy planes shoot our planes down. We lose lives as well as letters. I pray that God will bring us together soon. Tell Sandra I love her.

Always yours,
Nicky

555th Parachute Battalion

In the early years of the war, African-American soldiers served primarily in non-combat roles, but two years after the Japanese attack on Pearl Harbor, African-Americans were training in a variety of combat units. On December 30, 1943, at Fort Benning, the 555th Infantry Battalion of the 101st Airborne Division was activated. It was an African-American unit with African-American officers. All members were volunteers, and the enlisted cadre was selected from the 92nd Infantry Division at Fort Huachuca, Arizona, home of the Buffalo Soldiers. The 555th did not serve overseas during World War II, but carried out missions fighting fires in the Pacific Northwest. The 555th earned the name "Smoke Jumpers."

Many African-American soldiers passed for white so that they could serve in combat units overseas. Anatole Broyard, a *New York Times* book critic, was one of an estimated 150,000 African-American soldiers who enlisted as white men. Not until the end of the war were African-American soldiers allowed to fight in racially integrated units.

January 1944

To prepare for the invasion of the continent, Allied air forces began dropping arms and supplies to French, Belgian, and Italian partisans. "The Battle of Berlin" began. The term referred to the heaviest, most concentrated bomb attack the city would experience.

In London, General Eisenhower met with other Allied Expeditionary Force commanders to plan Operation Overlord, the landing of Allied troops in France.

Hitler expected the Allies to invade France at the Pas de Calais, and the area was one of the most heavily defended places on the coast. Allied commanders decided to attack the more lightly defended Normandy beaches.

To disguise their intent, strategists planned Operation Fortitude, the creation of a phantom U.S. 1st Army under the command of General George C. Patton and a simulated build-up of arms near the Straits of Dover. "Tanks" and "Landing Ship Tanks" made of rubber, canvas, and plywood were photographed by German reconnaissance, and the deception was successful.

★ ★ ★ ★ ★ ★ ★ ★ ★ ★ ★ ★ ★

January 9, 1944
Dearest Opal,

It has been about two weeks since I wrote. I've been away, and I just returned. I would like to tell you where I've been, but that is impossible. I certainly missed receiving mail, but when I got back to camp, I had seventeen letters from you, one from Dot, and three from New York. I got the colored pictures of you and Sandra. They look so real I feel like I could almost reach out my hand and touch both of you.

We have been working hard all day and all night, and I am having a terrible time just keeping my eyes open. I wrote to let you know that I am all right. I'll have a few days off, and I'll write you a longer letter.

I love you,
Nicky

January 12, 1944
Darling Opal,

Today I received the package with the handkerchiefs, the lighter, the cigarette case, and the wallet. But Darling, you should not have bought me such a fine case and lighter. I can use matches. After all, matches were invented before cigarette lighters.

How is our daughter? By now, she must be a big girl. Watch out; soon she'll be going out with boys. All kidding aside, I'd love to see her. Do you think that she will let me hold her when I come home?

Your Loving Husband,
Nicky

January 13, 1944
Dearest Opal,

The weather here has changed since I first arrived. We don't get much rain, but it sure is cold.

The lighter you sent me works well, and I like the cigarette case and wallet. I put the pictures you sent in frames, and I am lying here looking at them.

I'd give everything I have for just a glimpse of you and Sandra.

Honey, the company is restricted, so I can't go to town to have a picture made, but I'll do it the first chance I get. I love you.

Good night Darling,

Nicky

January 14, 1944

Dear Opal,

The weather here is very cold. It's so foggy that you can't see 100 yards in front of you. The fog muffles sound too, and it's very quiet here . . . .

I like to imagine the day when I come home. You'll buy yourself a new outfit and look your prettiest. Sandra will be as beautiful, fresh, and sweet as a rose. You'll be standing tall and proud, but you'll be a little nervous like you always were when you met me at the train station.

I love you.

Nicky

January 15, 1944

Dear Opal,

I am the envy of all the boys in the company. I have more handkerchiefs than anybody else. The food is better, but I still don't like it. I haven't eaten a fried egg since I got here.

It seems like only yesterday that we were dating. Then we were married, and now we have a baby to add to our joy. Soon the war will end, and I'll come home to you. Good night, Darling.

I love you.

Nicky

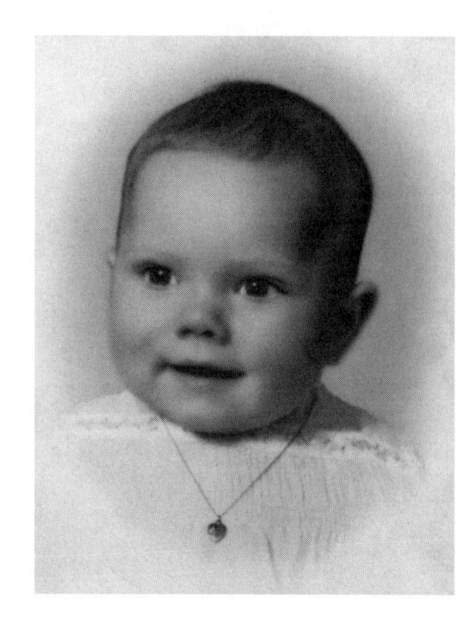

Baby Sandra

Invasion of Anzio

Allied commanders believed a landing at Anzio on the central coast of Italy was necessary to take Rome and to establish lines of attack on southern France. On January 22, the 504th, the 509th, and three battalions of rangers led the attack. To prepare for the invasion, Allied air forces flew more than 1,200 sorties against light anti-aircraft fire. Lt. Col. William O. Darby led his Rangers across minefields to seize the port of Anzio, and the 509th occupied Nettuno. The Allies wanted to establish a strong beachhead from which to attack north, but during a week of delays, German reinforcements rushed to the area. Darby's Rangers lost most of the 1st and 3rd Battalions, about 800 men, near Cisterna. U.S. forces remained isolated near Anzio for four months until May when an Allied offensive pushed north.

★ ★ ★ ★ ★ ★ ★ ★ ★ ★ ★ ★ ★

January 24, 1944
Dear Opal,

I received the snapshots. The baby is pretty, and I am very proud of her and her lovely mother. Patricia has grown; she's a big girl. I'd like to see her and Dot. I am glad that Sandra has a sweet little cousin to play with . . . .

I love you.
Nicky

January 25, 1944
Dear Opal,

How are you and the baby? As I write this letter, I'm looking at your picture. I miss the baby although I've never seen her. I didn't receive letters today, but I did receive the razor blades, and Gee, Darling, I didn't need that many razor blades. They will probably last me for the next six months. . . .

Goodnight, Darling. I look far into the future, and I see only happiness for the three of us.

Always yours,
Nicky

January 26, 1944
Dearest Opal,

Today I received your letters written January 12 and 13. I've written every day since I came back from that trip, but as I said, sometimes the letters just don't get through. I know you feel terrible when you don't get mail, because that's the way I feel. . . .

February 1, Bing Crosby and Frank Sinatra will have a singing contest staged just for troops overseas. Who do you think will win?

I love you.

Nicky

January 27, 1944

Dear Opal,

Remember how I used to think of you every night at 8:00 P.M.? I don't do that anymore. Now I think of you all the time. I talk about you, and I dream about you. Darling, send pictures of you and Sandra whenever you can.

Love always,

Nicky

February 1944

Russian forces defeated German troops in several battles along the eastern front, and the U.S.S.R took control of the coast of the Gulf of Finland. R.A.F. planes attacked targets in Limoges, France. Flying Fortresses and B-25s dropped 400 tons of bombs on Monte Cassino, the abbey in Italy founded by St. Benedict in 529 A.D. The Allies began massive barrages over Germany.

★ ★ ★ ★ ★ ★ ★ ★ ★ ★ ★ ★ ★

February 2, 1944

Dear Opal,

I'm dying to see our little girl. When I come home, do you think Sandra will recognize me? Tell me about Sandra. Is her hair still red? Are her eyes still blue? Does she still laugh all the time? You said she doesn't like water. She is like her Mom and Dad. They don't like water either. Maybe if you put a highball or a Cuba Libre in her bottle, she would like it better.

If either of you gets sick, no matter what a trifle it might seem, go to the doctor. I think I would go completely crazy if anything happened to either of you.

Today I visited Roger Gray, and I was pleased to meet him. He just returned from two weeks on special duty. I showed him pictures of you and Sandra and Mary Dean [Gray] and Scarlett [Mary Dean and Roger Gray's daughter] and do you know what? He wanted to keep my pictures! But I didn't let him have them. I told him you will have copies made. Will you, Hon?

General Montgomery visited our camp and spoke to the troops. He is quite a talker.

You asked me how old I am. When we were married, I was 28 and now I'm 30. I was born January 7, 1914. Mrs. Bonilla, I know I'm a daddy, and the baby will soon be calling me Papa, but I'm not an old man.

I got a calendar from Rev. Cantrell, and I continue to get pamphlets from him. I sent you some English newspapers and a book. A picture of me is in the book. Send me a Birmingham newspaper when you get a chance. I'd like to know what's going on down there. Thanks for the pictures. Patricia is really growing.

If you don't hear from me or about me for a while, remember, "No news is good news."

I wish I could take you out to dinner, dancing, or walking. I know you get lonely and bored. When you are blue, take Sandra's little face in your hands, look into her eyes, and think of me. Maybe then, you won't feel so lonely.

Always Yours,
Nicky

February 3, 1944
Darling Opal,

Is everything all right with you and Sandra? I never knew I could love anyone as much as I love you. Tell those handsome brothers of yours I said to take care of you.

Always yours,
Nicky

February 4, 1944
Dear Opal,

Today, snow fell for the first time since I've been here, but it didn't last long, only for about an hour. I am writing this while I'm waiting to eat, just thinking about you and the baby. I want to send you something from England. What would you like?

Always yours,
Nicky

February 23, 1944
Dear Opal,

Today I received ten airmail letters and eleven V-mail letters. The pictures of Sandra, Patricia, and Farris are good. I like the one where Farris is holding Sandra and Patricia is kissing her. I know they love each other, and I love you for taking such good care of our daughter.

Dad certainly looks good in his uniform. Why, I was kidding the boys, and I told them that my dad-in-law, as old as he is, looks better in uniform than they do. After I showed them the picture, they admitted that he looks good. I didn't tell them that he is a watchman at the war plant. I told them that he is in the army and, Darling, they believed me.

Mary Dean Gray is an attractive girl. Richard gave me four pictures that she sent. And thank you for the Valentine. It was the sweetest Valentine I have ever seen. I am going to keep it and take it with me wherever I go.

Did you get Sandra a baby carriage? Does she like it? A long time ago, you told me you were a spendthrift. I know you're more careful now that you have Sandra and me.

Of course, Sandra is the most beautiful baby in Irondale. Anybody who says she isn't will have to answer to me.

Darling, about two months ago, I wrote to my mother, and told her that you and I were married and we have a baby. I've received five letters from her, but she has never mentioned you or the baby, so I've stopped writing to her. I received a letter from my uncle asking for a picture of you and the baby, so I sent him three. He said to tell you that you did not get a bargain when you got me.

Have to close now. Sirens sounding; lights off. It's an air raid warning. Since I'm watching my daughter grow up in pictures, please send as many as possible.

Love always,
Nicky

February 28, 1944
Dearest Opal,

How is our delightful daughter?

The weather here is still cold, and we get an occasional flurry of snow, but not much rain.

Remember that singing contest between Bing Crosby and Frank Sinatra? Bing Crosby won. Then Frank Sinatra challenged Dick Haymes. Guess who won? Bing Crosby, and he wasn't even in the contest. Sinatra demanded a re-match with Crosby, and Crosby won again.

Why do I love you so much? In my mind, I relive the last days we spent together. My heart aches for you.

I try to write long letters like I did when I was at Fort Bragg, and I'd like to tell you more, but I can't. The censors would cross out anything specific I might say. Even if you don't hear from me for a long time, know that I am all right.

Love always,
Nicky

March 1944

German armies occupied Hungary and in daylight raids on Berlin, the 8th Air Force lost 80 aircraft and crews. Frankfurt and Stuttgart were bombed. Allies blasted Nuremburg, but 95 planes were lost and 71 were damaged.

Nicky sent Opal newspaper clippings about training in England. The March 24, 1944, issue of *Stars and Stripes* reported a demonstration jump in the south of England:

CHURCHILL, EISENHOWER WATCH SKY SHOW BY AIRBORNE YANKS
By Philip W. Bucknell

Prime Minister Winston Churchill and Gen. Dwight D. Eisenhower yesterday inspected a combined paratroop and glider-borne unit, whose men are, in the Prime Minister's words, "the most modern expression of war."

While the two were inspecting ranks of heavily armed troops, other soldiers were boarding planes for a demonstration mass jump . . . a powerful epilogue to the show.

At the conclusion of the formal inspection, troopers and glider riders were invited to break ranks and form a semi-circle around the leaders. Cowboy yells and shouts of "Geronimo" sang out.

To them, the Prime Minister said: "I see gathered here on English soil these soldiers of our great American ally preparing themselves to strike a blow for. . . a greater cause than either of the two countries have ever fought for. Soon you will have the opportunity of testifying your faith in all those inspiring phrases of the American Constitution, and of striking a blow which . . . will make it a better and broader world for all. I thank God you are here, and from the bottom of my heart wish you all good fortune and success."

Nicky also sent an article dated March 25, 1944, about the Luftwaffe bombing London.

LONDON HAS ALL-FIRE RAID NIGHT; MASSED GUNS MEET BOMBER WAVES
By Daily Mail Reporter

Waves of German bombers attacked London last night in one of the sharpest all-fire raids on the Capital since the blitz. High-explosive bombs were dropped in some areas, but the attack was apparently aimed at fire-raising. The raiders came in from the northwest and from the southeast. Aircraft flying high from the south to the northeast ran into a heavy barrage. There were few searchlights, but the flashes of the shell bursts could be seen following the path of the planes. Incendiaries were in one Central London area. Hundreds of fireguards were in action and they were helped by the new N.F.S. [National Fire Service] roof-spotting system . . . .

Exercise Beaver

From March 27 through March 31, the 101st participated in Exercise Beaver. Civilians evacuated Slapton Sands near the British port of Torquay, and Allied troops carried out amphibious operations. Slapton Sands beaches were long and narrow, separated from the mainland by a shallow lake and marshland, and connected by two causeways. The topography of the area was similar to that of Utah Beach. Soldiers rode trains or trucks to simulated drop zones, and they were scattered, as they would have been in a real jump. The 502nd captured the bridges leading inland, and they secured a simulated 155-mm gun position. Enemy reconnaissance and intelligence reported each maneuver as an invasion, and German commanders were tense.

April 1944

In Rumania, the U.S. 15th Air Force began attacks against the Ploesti oilfields. Shortages of fuel would limit mobility of German troops and threaten production in war plants.

General Giraud resigned, and General Charles DeGaulle was appointed Commander-in-Chief of French armed forces in North Africa.

The U.S. Tactical Air Force began attacks on German artillery positions in Normandy.

★ ★ ★ ★ ★ ★ ★ ★ ★ ★ ★ ★ ★

April 1, 1944
My Darling Opal,

When I came in from the field this morning, I received seven letters from you, and a letter from our cousin Dotsy in California. I'm glad to make her acquaintance, if only in a letter. I received the *Birmingham News* dated February 28 and 29. Gee, that package took a long time to get here. I know I haven't written often, but sometimes, it is impossible . . . .

Today I washed my clothes. I wish you had been here to tell me how to do it. I put all my dirty clothes, coveralls, underwear, socks, and field jacket in one pail and boiled the dickens out of them. What a mess! Everything changed color. I'll have to get some new clothes

How is our little girl? Opal, I lie awake at night wondering how you and Sandra would be cared for if something happened to me. I love you both so much that sometimes I wish we had never met. But then I would never have known the happiness of having a wife and baby. Late at night when everyone is asleep, I cry because I can't be with you. If I should go to meet my maker, I would continue to love you. I know I'll come home soon, and I'll do everything I can to make you happy.

You say my mother would be ready to forgive us for marrying without her approval if she saw Sandra. I'll tell you what to do, if you have the nerve. Go to New York and see her, and tell me what happens. I am 3,000 miles away, so maybe I won't hear her yell. If you agree to go, I'll make preparations. *[Opal never met any of Nicky's family.]*

Tell Mom I love her, and I appreciate everything she does for you and Sandra. Tell Dad I was asking for him.

Always yours,

Nicky

April 2, 1944

Darling Opal,

Today I received your letters dated March 14 and March 20. You say your letters are dull. All you do is stay home, go the post office, and take Sandra for a walk. That is just what I want to hear. I don't want to hear that you're dining in Birmingham's best restaurants and dancing the night away in nightclubs. Remember, I am the jealous type, and you are somebody to be jealous about.

For the last two weeks, I've dreamed about you every night. Before I go to sleep, I lie in the dark and think of you. I remember the wonderful days we lived together in Fayetteville. I was so happy then, and I am so sad now. When I heard that Sandra had been born, I was walking on air. Now I can hardly make it through the day because I want to see her so much.

How would you like to have maybe eight or nine more babies? I'll build a big house for my big family. Sandra is saying "Daddy" already? She is only eight months old. Maybe she'll be as smart as the "Quiz Kids." I am going to London this week, and I'll try to have a picture made.

Take care of my girls. No one could ever love the two of you as much as I do.

Happy Birthday, Darling. Did you think I forgot? I'll be with you next year.

Love always,

Nicky

April 3, 1944

Dear Opal,

Hello, Darling. How is the baby? Still full of life? I want her to be a big girl like her mother. She is already sweet and pretty, just like her mother. I know she will grow up to be a fine woman.

I wish I could bring you both to England. I would take you to see Buckingham Palace, the Tower of London, and Big Ben. We would ride a red double-deck bus and then take the train to Scotland. We would go to Ireland. We would visit the towns and villages where the Keiths lived before they came to the U.S. We'd find a hundred more relatives.

I love you.

Nicky

April 4, 1944

Dear Mom,

Remember me? I'm your new son-in-law, the one who never writes. But Mom, I'll try to do better. I can still taste the good meal you cooked for me, and I'm looking forward to eating another one soon.

Mom, are Opal and Sandra too much trouble? I hope not. I know if Sandra is like her dad, she is at least a little trouble.

Mom, you are the sweetest Mom-in-law any man could have, and I love you for caring for my wife and baby.

Your son,
Nicky

April 4, 1944
Dear Dad,

Did anyone ever tell you that you are a fine looking man in uniform? I'm not kidding. Everyone who sees your picture says so. The boys of the company say I should be proud to have a father-in-law in the Army.

Yes, Dad, the boys think you're in the army.

Dad, are you still taking that cold medicine you make? [John Keith made "cough syrup,"—rock candy dissolved in rye whiskey.] I'll bet that stuff is really good for a cold.

Do you like your new granddaughter? Does she look like a Keith or does she look like a Bonilla? I'd rather she look like a Keith. You are a good-looking family.

Dad, what kind of souvenir would you like me to bring you? Let me know, and I'll get it.

Your son,
Nicky

April 4, 1944
Dear James,

How are all the girls in Irondale? Have you found the right one, or are you still playing the field? Opal said you had to quit your job because you're still having trouble with your stomach. That's too bad. I hope you'll get completely well soon.

Say, don't ever come to England if you don't have to. The girls over here are not much to look at. They have awful shapes.

Regards,
Nicky

April 4, 1944
Dear Fred,

Hello Fred, Do you remember me? I hope you do. How is your job? Do you like it? Opal says you're thinking about joining the Navy. Don't do it. The Army, Navy, and Marines are all the same—tough on the enlisted men. Consider joining the Merchant Marines. It's a good outfit. You will learn a trade, get good pay, and travel. Think it over, and keep your chin up.

Regards,
Nicky

Fred Keith in his Navy uniform

[Fred was eligible for the draft, and he reasoned that if he served on a ship, he would have a roof over his head and a clean, dry place to sleep. He would be able to bathe, to eat cooked food rather than K-rations, and he would not have to dig latrines or foxholes. He joined the U. S. Navy.]

April 4, 1944
Dear Dot,

Thank you for the letters. It is nice to know that you think of me. I'm sorry I haven't answered, but I promise to be a better correspondent. Say, I got some cute pictures of Patricia and Sandra. The one where Patricia is kissing Sandra is very sweet. Opal tells me that you're working. Do you like your job?

Love,
Nicky

Exercise Tiger

In April, Exercise Tiger, a live ammunition maneuver at Slapton Sands, involved 300 ships and 30,000 men. The 101st rode trucks to an area behind the beach simulating a night drop. They attacked fortifications from behind.

Observing from aboard ship, General Eisenhower saw that things were going wrong. Air cover failed, landing craft were late, and fire from tanks wounded Allied troops. Three L.S.T.s were to hit the beaches as they would hit Utah Beach in Normandy during the invasion, but on April 28, German torpedo boats sank two of these L.S.T.s, and 749 soldiers and 197 sailors were killed. Commanders ordered survivors not to discuss the incident, but they feared that other soldiers might have been captured, interrogated, and forced to reveal what they knew of plans for the invasion.

★ ★ ★ ★ ★ ★ ★ ★ ★ ★ ★ ★ ★

April 20, 1944
Dearest Opal,

Darling, I was away for a couple of weeks and I couldn't write until I got back to my permanent station. I did receive mail, and I got an airmail letter only seven days after you mailed it. Fast, wasn't it?

I can hardly believe that I have you and Sandra waiting for me. I received the new pictures of Sandra, and she is growing fast.

I know you looked pretty on Easter Sunday wearing your new dress. I'll bet you looked like the ideal modern mother.

Your letters are precious to me. Never stop writing, no matter how long it is before you hear from me. I'd like to tell you more, but I can't.

I wanted to send Mom flowers, but I couldn't. I couldn't even go to town to buy a present. I don't have much of an opportunity to spend money, so I'm sending a couple hundred dollars. Give my love to all the family.

Love always,
Nicky

April 21, 1944
Darling Opal,

Didn't get mail today, but guess I'll get two letters tomorrow . . . . Opie, you always ask what I want or need. Well, Darling, please send me a pair of Sandra's shoes. I want to wear them around my neck when I go into action. I know they will bring me luck.

Forever yours,
Nicky

May 1944

On May 8, General Eisenhower set June 5 as the date for the invasion of Normandy. The mission of the 101st was to capture Carentan and to link Utah and Omaha beaches. The U.S. 8th Air Force attacked French airfields to destroy as many German aircraft as possible. Despite the threat of invasion, the German government used limited resources to send sixty-two railway trucks filled with Jews from Hungary to concentration camps in Poland.

Exercise Eagle

Exercise Eagle, May 9-12, in the Wilts area of Hungerford and Newbury, was as close to the real thing as the 101st would experience until D-Day. Taking off from the same airports they would use for the invasion, troops jumped from airplanes to secure a causeway leading away from a beach simulating Normandy beaches. Most of the division jumped at the wrong coordinates, and many troopers were injured, but the mission was considered a success.

On May 11, Axis Sally, an American actress named Mildred Sisk Gillars, played the lead role in "Vision of Invasion," a drama broadcast to American troops. Sally had been broadcasting German propaganda for Radio Berlin since December 1941. This May evening, Sally acted the part of an American mother who dreams that her son dies aboard a burning ship attempting to cross the English Channel in an invasion of France. Sound effects included gunfire, bomb bursts, and moans and cries of the wounded. At the end of the radio play, an announcer said, "D-Day stands for doom, disaster, death, defeat. . . . " [9]

★ ★ ★ ★ ★ ★ ★ ★ ★ ★ ★ ★ ★

May 12, 1944
Darling Opal,

I just returned to camp from the field. I received sixteen V-mail letters and seven airmail letters. I opened the airmail letters first because I thought they might have pictures in them. I was thrilled to see you pushing Sandra in her baby carriage. In one picture, your skirt is blowing up just a little, and you look so young and sweet.

I kiss your picture every night. If I'm in camp, I kiss the big one, but if I'm in the field, I kiss the one in my wallet. I show everyone I meet my pictures of you and Sandra. Here is how I do it. I ask, "Would you like to see pictures of my little family?" And if someone says yes, I show the latest ones. Everyone says that I have a cute baby, and then I say, "You're telling me?"

The pictures I had made for you finally arrived. I'll send them in two packages and hope you'll get at least one set. Forgive me for not writing a long letter tonight. I don't think I've ever written you a fifteen-page letter, so that's what I'll do tomorrow. Good night.

I love you.
Nicky

May 23, 1944
Dear Opal,

I received your letters of May 16 and 17. Fast time, isn't it? How is our daughter? I know she is getting the best care from a loving mother . . . .

Please send me some food: hot green peppers in jars, pickled herring, cheese, salami, etc. I might have use for it. Good night, Darling. Give my love to the family.

I am forever yours.

Nicky

May 24, 1944

Dearest Opal,

When you receive this letter, I hope you are in good health and as sweet as you always are. Gee, Honey, I miss you so much. I wish I could be with you right at this very moment, but even though I am not with you in person, I know that I am with you in spirit. Opie, I sure like that little colored picture of Sandra . . . .

I love you, Darling, and will always continue to love you no matter what happens, and when I come home, I'm never going to leave your side, not for all the money in the world.

Goodnight,

Nicky

May 30, 1944

Darling Opal,

I'm sitting here watching a boy have all his hair cut off, and I'm wondering whether to have mine cut. If I do, I won't have to comb it, and it will be more comfortable and easier to keep clean.

I was thinking about returning all the pictures you have sent me, but when things look glum, I will need those pictures to boost my morale. If you do not hear from me for a long time, just remember that you will always be on my mind and in my heart, no matter where I am.

Darling, there is so much I want to say, but the words won't come. I don't know what's the matter. My thoughts are all jumbled up like a jigsaw puzzle. I'm having a hard time putting the pieces together. But the most important piece of the puzzle is my love for you. I love you more than you'll ever know.

Darling, the first Sunday after you receive this letter, go to church and say a prayer for the boys.

Always yours,

Nicky

Countdown to D-Day

In the Pacific, the Battle of the Philippine Sea destroyed many Japanese aircraft carriers and planes.

American and British spies in France gathered intelligence about troop placements and resistance efforts and radioed the information to coordinate D-Day drops. Virginia Hall, a young woman from Baltimore, Maryland, working in France for the U.S. Office of Strategic Services, later named the Central Intelligence Agency, disguised herself as an elderly milkmaid and broadcast information to Americans. The Gestapo circulated a wanted poster naming Virginia Hall as one of the most dangerous Allied agents in France, one who must be found and destroyed. For her work, Hall, a civilian, was awarded the Distinguished Service Cross.

Violette Bushnell, daughter of an English father and a French mother, married a French Lieutenant, Etienne Szabo. When he was killed at El Alamein in North Africa, she became a spy for the British. She parachuted into France in April 1944 and relayed information to the Allies until she was captured by the Gestapo and executed in 1945.

Cpl. Charles Chibitty, one of seventeen Comanche tribe members who served in the Army's Signal Corps, sent messages about the invasion in his language, one that German cryptographers never decoded. Allied leaders feared that the German intelligence might learn about the invasion and communicate plans with their own network of spies and cryptographers.

Marshaling area in England before D-Day
National Archives

On May 31, men of the 101st moved to airfields where they were isolated behind barbed wire fences and guarded by sentries with machine guns. No one could get in or out unless authorized. Soldiers wrote letters home and listened to band concerts. They cleaned their weapons and sharpened their knives. They studied maps, aerial photographs, and scale models of Normandy beaches and the drop zones behind them.

British Air Vice-Marshals Arthur Tedder and Trafford Leigh-Mallory feared the 101st might suffer seventy-percent casualties. Concerned about such a possibility, General Eisenhower spent many days before the invasion visiting men in the field. He wanted every man who would go across on D-Day to see the man who was sending him into battle. He talked to hundreds personally in the four months between February 1 and June 1. He visited twenty-six divisions, twenty-four airfields, five war ships, and countless depots, shops, hospitals, and other installations. The invasion, planned for June 5, was delayed because of weather. General Eisenhower decided that the invasion would begin after midnight on June 6.

At 6:00 P. M. on June 5, Eisenhower and a group of aides drove to Newbury where some soldiers of the 101st were preparing to board planes for the flight across the Atlantic. Eisenhower wandered around through groups of men who camouflaged their faces with ashes, soot from plane exhaust, or burnt cork. Soldiers did not want Nazi defenders to see their white faces in the darkness of the French countryside. Some troopers shaved their heads "Indian style" leaving a strip of hair through the middle. Some wore war paint. When men recognized Eisenhower, they gathered around and chatted.

General Eisenhower told the men of the 101st that they were the best-trained, best-equipped, and best-led troops he had ever seen. He told them not to worry. One man replied, "Hell, we ain't worried, General. It's the Krauts that ought to be worrying now." Another man called out, "Look out Hitler; here we come."[10] Eisenhower stayed at the airfield until the last C-47 roared into the air.

In a letter from France, Nicky said that Eisenhower spoke to him, that his face was blackened, and that his picture was taken. He told Opal to look for the photograph. Opal saved two copies of Signal Corps photo number 194399. She identified Nicky as the soldier farthest back under the visor of General Eisenhower's cap. The true identity of the soldiers in the photograph continues to be a matter of dispute.

General Eisenhower talks to men of the 101st Airborner Division prior to their drop into Europe on D-Day. Nicky may be the soldier just under Eisenhower's hat brim.
National Archives

Chapter Six

D-Day and War in France

June 1944

Operation Overlord was the code name for the invasion of Nazi-occupied France. In twenty-four hours, 175,000 troops and their equipment including artillery, jeeps, motorcycles, tanks, and armored bulldozers were moved sixty to one hundred miles across the English Channel and landed in hostile territory against fierce opposition. The fate of Europe would be decided on this day. If Field Marshal Rommel could stall the invasion at the Atlantic Wall. the German coastline defenses, tanks could speed to the points of attack and drive Allied forces back into the sea.

American soldiers were in top physical condition, highly trained, and well equipped, but most had never seen combat. Some military leaders, including Hitler, questioned whether Britain or the United States could produce soldiers as good as Germany's best.

Troops filed onto their transports and landing craft, and commanders read Eisenhower's Order of the Day:

> Soldiers, sailors, and airmen of the Allied Expeditionary Force: You are about to embark upon the Great Crusade toward which we have striven these months. The eyes of the world are upon you. You will bring about the destruction of the German war machine, the elimination of Nazi tyranny over oppressed peoples of Europe, and security for ourselves in a free world. The hope and prayers of liberty-loving people everywhere march with you . . . . Your task will not be an easy one. Your enemy is well trained, well equipped, and battle- hardened. He will fight savagely. But this is the year 1944.
>
> Much has happened since the Nazi triumphs of 1940-41 . . . . The tide has turned.
>
> The free men of the world are marching together to victory. I have full confidence in your courage, devotion to duty, and skill in battle. We will accept nothing less than full victory.

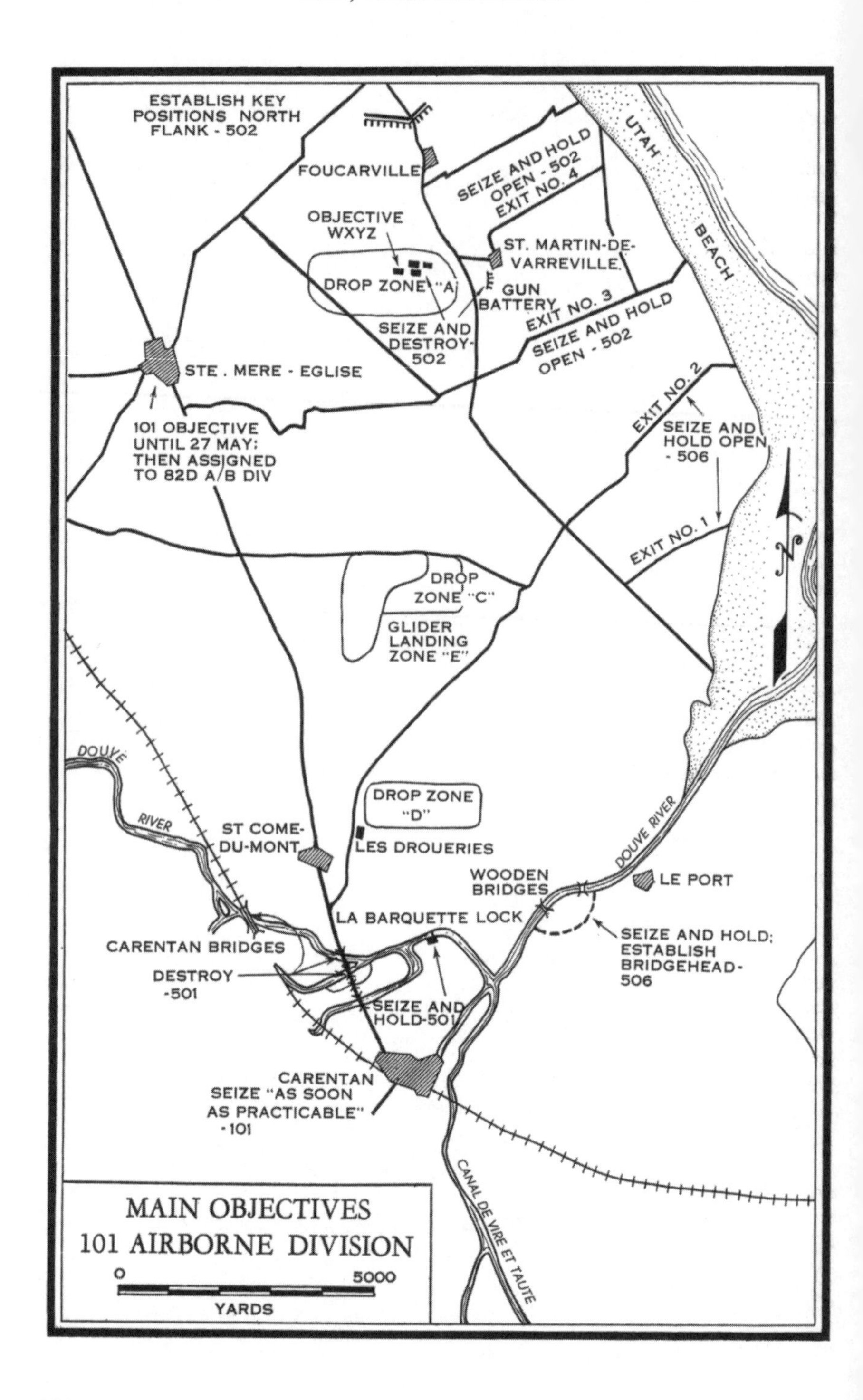
ESTABLISH KEY POSITIONS NORTH FLANK - 502
FOUCARVILLE
SEIZE AND HOLD OPEN - 502 EXIT NO. 4
UTAH BEACH
OBJECTIVE WXYZ
ST. MARTIN-DE-VARREVILLE
DROP ZONE "A"
GUN BATTERY
EXIT NO. 3
SEIZE AND HOLD OPEN - 502
SEIZE AND DESTROY-502
STE. MERE - EGLISE
EXIT NO. 2
SEIZE AND HOLD OPEN - 506
101 OBJECTIVE UNTIL 27 MAY: THEN ASSIGNED TO 82D A/B DIV
EXIT NO. 1
N
DROP ZONE "C"
GLIDER LANDING ZONE "E"
DOUVE
RIVER
DROP ZONE "D"
ST COME-DU-MONT
LES DROUERIES
DOUVE RIVER
WOODEN BRIDGES
LE PORT
LA BARQUETTE LOCK
SEIZE AND HOLD; ESTABLISH BRIDGEHEAD-506
CARENTAN BRIDGES
DESTROY -501
SEIZE AND HOLD-501
CARENTAN SEIZE "AS SOON AS PRACTICABLE" -101
CANAL DE VIRE ET TAUTE
MAIN OBJECTIVES 101 AIRBORNE DIVISION
0
5000
YARDS

Good Luck.

And let us all beseech the blessings of almighty God upon this great and noble undertaking.

["Order of the Day Issued by Gen. Eisenhower" Birmingham Post, June 6, 1944]

Most of the 502nd flew in C-47s from the 88th Troop Carrier squadron. They were among the first groups departing from Greenham Common. Aircraft flew from the west over the Channel Islands hoping to avoid heavy anti-aircraft fire in the skies over Cherbourg. General Maxwell Taylor flew with the 502nd, which was commanded by Colonel George Van Horn Moseley. Darkness and clouds covered the Cherbourg Peninsula of France, bullets riddled the planes, and fiery bursts of flak exploded everywhere. Pilots were forced to open formations to avoid collisions and antiaircraft fire. Drops were badly scattered, and most dropped artillery pieces were lost.

Troopers could shed their parachutes in thirty seconds, but bad landings could knock them unconscious. A battalion needed about an hour to form for attack. Many troopers were shot as they descended. Some drowned in flooded meadow-lands; some were shot while they were mired in marshes. The hedgerows, rock and dirt barriers planted with trees, provided good cover for German soldiers. In the first hours of the invasion, approximately 1,400 Allied paratroopers were killed or captured.

In an undated story from *Yank*, Second Lt. Samuel S. Cromie, a pilot, described the drop from his plane:

> [The] men were smoking a lot and drinking a lot of water . . . . A lot of them were praying all the way over, kneeling on the floor . . . . When we pulled in over the Peninsula, we found a perfect cover of clouds there, which kept us away from the fire on the ground. Then, just as we started in over the D.Z. [drop zone], the bullets and the flak started coming up at us again, in every color of the rainbow. We gave the men the red light warning, showing that we were four minutes from the DZ. . . . [We] slowed down for the drop, gave them the green light, and out they went . . . . Guns were meeting our paratroopers as they dropped, following them all the way to the ground."

In the jump, Col. Moseley broke his leg. He ordered soldiers to put him in a wheelbarrow and push him toward the front. He wanted to remain in the action, but General Taylor ordered him to relinquish command of the 502nd to Col. John C. (Mike) Michaelis. The 506th captured southerly exits designated 1 and 2, and the 502nd captured northerly exits designated 3 and 4 of causeways leading inland across marshes behind Utah beach. Causeway number 4 ran through the village of St. Martin-de-Varreville and through a position designated WXYZ.

The July 1944 issue of *Yank* magazine.

Staff Sergeant Harrison Summers of B Company, 1st Battalion, led an attack that captured the position. At the end of D-Day, soldiers of the 502nd and the 4th Infantry Division were protecting the northern flank of the three lower causeways. 1st and 2nd Battalions of the 501st captured bridgheads over the Douve River.

During the following days, the 101st met strong Nazi resistance, but the paratroopers seized Pouppeville, and St. Come du Mont. On June 12, the division seized Carentan, the largest town of the Cherbourg Peninsula, and nearby railheads and highways. After the battle, soldiers called the Carentan Causeway "Purple Heart Lane." Soldiers of the 101st fought in the area until June 27 when they were relieved and sent to Cherbourg. There they remained in reserve until mid-July.

"Are You Real?" Army Nurses

After medics had given immediate aid, Army nurses cared for men of the 101st in training camps and evacuation hospitals; they served under fire on hospital trains, ships, and planes. After D-Day, nurses crossed the English Channel in L.S.T.s escorted by Allied fighter planes. In *No Time for Fear*, Army nurse Mary Ferrell described landing on Utah Beach and marching several miles inland. In a tent pitched in an apple orchard, she and a friend slept on one raincoat with another raincoat as a cover. The next day, they were trucked to the 35th Evacuation Hospital.

Ferrell worked at the 35th in Normandy with limited equipment until General Patton's 3rd Army became operational on August 1. The hospital staff followed battles, picking up wounded, treating them, and carrying them along to the next battle.

Ferrell remembers when Marlene Dietrich visited her hospital:

> She sang "Lili Marlene" and "The Boys in the Backroom" for the patients in the wards. She changed clothes in my tent, arriving in army fatigues, then appearing in the wards in a very shiny, sparkling, long gown. She was beautiful and would always show the calf of her leg to the patients as she left. [Then the boys sang] the risqué song, "Roll Me Over."
>
> I'd like people to know how much I admired these boys. I would never have believed what they could take. It was the Army nurse's privilege to give the best nursing care possible to the sick and wounded soldiers. The words of a badly wounded young man. . . were thanks enough. "Are you real?" or "You are wonderful," or "You are here in hell with us."[11]

Mary Ferrell was awarded the Bronze Star for meritorious service, and she wore with great pride five campaign ribbons.

News from the Battlefields

American journalists and photographers came into Normandy in later amphibious and aircraft landings; they worked for *The New York Times*, *Stars and Stripes*, The Associated Press, United Press, *Colliers*, and other newspapers, radio networks, and magazines. Among reporters were Thomas Wolf, Edward R. Murrow, Walter Cronkite, Ernie Pyle, Andy Rooney, James Agee, Martha Gellhorn, Mary Welsh, and Ernest Hemingway. Martha Gellhorn hid in a bathroom on a hospital ship scheduled to cross the channel on June 7. Aboard the ship, she nursed the wounded, and that night, she went ashore with stretcher-bearers. She reached the beach before her husband and journalistic rival, Hemingway, who was still in a landing ship.

Government censors reviewed everything journalists wrote, and material considered detrimental to the war effort was forbidden. Reporters and photographers were not to present incompetence or irrationality. Crimes committed by G.I.s, and brawls over race and ethnicity were not to be reported. Stories and pictures of dead civilians, especially the elderly and children, and atrocities committed by Allied troops were censored, as were reports of Allied soldiers killed by fire from Allied forces.

In September 1943, *Life* magazine ran its first photos of American soldiers killed in New Guinea with a full-page editorial explaining that, as tragic as these deaths were, they were necessary if the Allies were to win the war.

Bill Mauldin's cartoons of Willie and Joe, battle-weary infantrymen, told the truth about the brutality of combat, usually with great irony, as did George

Baker's cartoon character the Sad Sack. Such information from the front was often all that families back home knew about those they loved who were in danger in far-away places.

Opal read news of the invasion in the June 6, 1944, *Birmingham Post.*

> TWO INVASION BEACHHEADS ARE CAPTURED IN FRANCE; ALLIES DRIVE INTO EUROPE NEAR HARVE
>
> By United Press
>
> Allied armies today stormed Northern France with history's greatest invasion armada—11,000 planes, 4,000 ships and thousands of smaller craft-and in the first few hours seized beachheads that threatened to isolate the Normandy Peninsula and win a railroad pointed straight at Paris. . . .

The front page of the *Birmingham Post* was filled with articles about the invasion:

> FIRST OF LANDING BARGES HITS BEACH 'ON THE MINUTE'
>
> EVERY YANK IN ATTACK IS AN 'ARSENAL'
>
> PASTORS OPEN CHURCHES FOR CITY'S PRAYER.
>
> GOV. *[Chauncey]* SPARKS URGES FAITH IN LEADERS.
>
> MORE *[coal]* MINES CLOSE *[in strikes]* ON INVASION DAY.
>
> *[Sgt. Alvin C.]* YORK *[World War I hero]* PREDICTS NAZI DEFEAT IN 60 DAYS
>
> FRENCH IN ALGIERS OVERJOYED BY NEWS

★ ★ ★ ★ ★ ★ ★ ★ ★ ★ ★ ★ ★

Hiding with her family in an attic in Amsterdam, fourteen-year-old Anne Frank heard news of the invasion on the B.B.C. She wrote her reaction to the news in her diary.

> A huge commotion in the Annex! Is this really the beginning of the long-awaited liberation? The liberation we've all talked so much about, which still seems too good, too much of a fairy tale, ever to come true? Will this year, 1944 bring us victory? We don't know yet, but where there's hope there's life. It fills us with fresh courage, and makes us strong again. We'll need to be brave to endure the many fears and hardships and the suffering to come . . . . [12]

★★★★★★★★★★★★★

WESTERN UNION

JUNE 7 INTL CD SANS ORIGINE
VIS VIA COMMERCIAL

MRS NICHOLAS L. BONILLA
1920 3RD AVE SOUTH
IRONDALE, ALA.

DARLING, ALL WELL AND SAFE. ALL MY LOVE DEAREST.

NICHOLAS BONILLA 8:07 AM

June 7, 1944
Darling Opal,

Just a few lines to let you know that everything is all right and that I am in pretty good health.

How are you Darling? Are you feeling all right; are you still losing weight; are you keeping yourself as beautiful as ever?

Darling, today has been a nice day; the sun was shining most of the time, it wasn't cold, and it looks like it will continue to stay nice.

Darling, I don't know if you notice[ed], but I always try to avoid writing about this darn war. I don't think you want to know more than you read *[in the newspapers]* and I don't care to speak to anyone at home about it.

Here are a few pictures and articles for the scrapbook. It should be pretty thick by now. We started it more than a year and a half ago.

Darling, if I ever write a letter and I don't say that I love you and I miss you, don't fret. I will always miss you when I'm away from you. Darling, I look at Sandra's picture at least four or five times a day, and when I look at her picture, I look at yours too. I wonder if Sandra will recognize me when I come home.

I am going to say goodnight until tomorrow when I will write again. Give my love to the family.

Always yours,
Nicky

★★★★★★★★★★★★★

About the soldiers who invaded France, poet Marianne Moore wrote, "[Their] spirits and . . . bodies were our shield, are still our shield."[13]

Lieutenant Colonel Robert G. Cole's 3rd Battalion

On June 10 and 11, the 502nd attacked German forces along the Carentan Causeway. Lt. Col. Robert G. Cole, leading 3rd Battalion of the 502nd, tried to force open the last of four bridges on the road to Carentan.

> [Suddenly] "his entire unit was . . . pinned to the ground by intense and withering enemy rifle, machinegun, mortar, and artillery fire. . . from heavily fortified positions within 150 yards. . . . After the devastating and unceasing enemy fire had for over an hour prevented any move and inflicted numerous casualties, Lt. Col. Cole, observing an almost helpless situation, courageously issued orders to assault the enemy positions with fixed bayonets.
>
> With utter disregard for his own safety, and completely ignoring the enemy fire, he rose to his feet in front of his battalion, and with drawn pistol shouted to his men to follow him in the assault. Catching up a fallen man's rifle and bayonet, he charged on and led the remnants of his battalion across the bullet-swept ground and into the enemy position. His heroic and valiant action in so inspiring his men resulted in the complete establishment of our bridgehead over the Douve River.[15]

For his actions, Lt. Col. Cole would be awarded the Medal of Honor.

General Eisenhower issued Communiqué No. 19 from London on June 15:

> On all parts of the front, all forces continue to carry the fight to the enemy. Heaviest fighting has taken place in the Carenten, Montebourg, and Caen areas. Airborne troops have successfully beaten off German attempts to retake Carentan and are again pushing southward from the town. They also advanced farther to the west in the Les Sablon-Baupte Vicinity."
>
> *[The Birmingham News]*

Sandra, Opal, Mary Dean and Scarlett

★★★★★★★★★★★★

June 17, 1944
Dearest Darling,

How are you? I hope you are in good health. I am all right.

Finally, I can tell you that I am in France, and I've seen quite a few Germans. France is a beautiful country. Vineyards and orchards grow along side the roads, and we get plenty of cider and wine. Cattle graze in fields nearby, and we buy all the milk, butter, and meat we want. I'm eating and drinking well and gaining weight.

I haven't received mail yet, but I should get some soon.

How are you and the baby? Is Sandra growing? Is she talking? I love you both. I'll write again as soon as I can.

All my love,
Nicky

(On American Red Cross stationery)
Sunday
June 18, 1943
5:00 P.M.
Darling Opal,

Just a line to let you know that I'm all right. As I told you before, we are in France and we have seen action many times. I am not going to say much about what we are doing here or what we have done because I know you don't want to hear about it.

Darling, I sure do miss you and the baby. I think of you all the time, night and day.

Right now, I'm lying in an apple orchard. The sun is shining bright, and I'm at peace with the world, writing to the sweetest person I know. . . . We have been buying all the meat we want, but it's impossible to get bread. The Germans took all the flour. I haven't received mail, but I hope to get some soon. Tell Sandra her daddy was asking for her. Give my love to the family.

Lovingly yours,
Nicky

A Salute from General William C. Lee

General William C. Lee, first commander of the 101st, had been sidelined by heart disease and replaced by General Maxwell Taylor. When Lee learned that his troops had led the invasion of France, he wrote a message for broadcast over Armed Forces Radio on June 20, 1944:

> For many months, men of the American 101st Airborne Division have trained for participation in the great Allied landings in France. Today these

> men have landed and are fighting in Normandy. They are physically hard and tough and mentally determined . . . .
>
> These airborne soldiers are imbued with the will to win regardless of any obstacles . . . . Their discipline is splendid. Their morale is high. Their absolute patriotism is unquestionable . . . . They are tough but kind. Hard but sympathetic . . . . They are generous in their feelings for the friendly people whose homelands are occupied by troops of the enemy. They are the sons and grandsons of men who fought in France in 1917-1918. From their fathers they have inherited admiration and respect for the ideals and aspirations of the democracies of the world . . . . [16]

Before D-Day, paratroopers had been told they would have to fight furiously for three days, and then they would be returned to England to prepare for the next jump. In reality, the 101st put in more than four weeks of hard fighting and suffered almost thirty-percent casualties.

Pulitzer Prize-winning poet Louis Simpson, who served with the 101st in France, Holland, Belgium, and Germany, wrote:

Carentan O Carentan
Before we met with you
We never yet had lost a man
Or known what death could do. [17]

On June 20, representative officers and men of the 101st assembled in the town square of Carentan, *Place de la Republique*. There, as General Maxwell Taylor awarded medals won in the campaign, German artillery rounds fell in the square, and soldiers and civilians ran for cover.

Men of the 101st Airborne Division in a French town.

★ ★ ★ ★ ★ ★ ★ ★ ★ ★ ★ ★

Sunday
June 25, 1944
8:00 P.M.
Darling Opal,

I have another chance to write, and I'm taking it. I'm in the best of health and hope you, the baby, and the rest of the family are well. Today I received the first mail since I jumped into France. Your letters were dated June 3, 4, 5, 6 and 8, and I was very happy to hear from you. Yes, Darling, the paratroopers have been doing an excellent job since we arrived here. In fact, every man in our Regiment has been decorated with the President's citation for heroic action. Isn't that swell?

Opie, here at the front we get only first class mail. We will get papers and packages when we are relieved and sent to a rest camp. I miss you and the baby. I look at your pictures at least three times a day. When I get back to the states, I am going to fall in love with you again. Goodnight. I hope I'll be able to write tomorrow.

My love for you is everlasting.
Always yours,
Nicky

502nd Unit Citation

The 502nd Parachute Infantry descended by parachute in the vicinity of *** [sic], France, on 6 June 1944. During the drop by parachute, the personnel of the regiment were spread in small groups and widely dispersed. Many casualties were sustained from heavy enemy fire from strongly fortified positions. Before the regiment was assembled, many fierce battles took place between small detachments and the enemy. Sometimes these groups were without officer or high-ranking noncommissioned officer.

Acts of gallantry and self-sacrifice were in evidence everywhere. The determination and bravery of the officers and enlisted men were inestimable. Many pillboxes, artillery emplacements, and fortified positions were reduced. The high ground commanding the landing beach was seized just prior to the landing of the assault waves of seaborne forces, and the strong enemy positions thereon reduced. Following this, the regiment seized the main causeways leading from the beach and held them until the arrival of the 4th Infantry Division.

The determined action of the 502nd Parachute Infantry made possible the successful landing and rapid advance inland of the seaborne assault troops, and assured the establishment of the Allied beachhead in France.

[U.S. War Department, the Adjutant General's Office.]

★★★★★★★★★★★

Monday
June 26, 1944
8:00 P. M.
Dear Opal,

Tonight it's raining, not very hard, but hard enough to make it miserable even though I am inside a building. I'm on outpost duty with two hours on and four hours off. But I don't get enough sleep. During those four hours, I have to eat, wash, clean my rifle, and do everything else . . . .

I would like to tell you about France and the things I have been doing, but it would never pass the censors. I guess you'll have to wait until I get home, and then I will tell you all about it.

I'm in good health, and I'm watching my step. Hope you and the baby are well. I'm certainly anxious to see both of you. Maybe I'll be home for Christmas. *[This hope might have been based on the fact that Cherbourg was liberated the following day, June 27.]* Wouldn't that be a magnificent gift for all of us?

Always,
Nicky

June 30, 1944
Dear Opal,

As I write this, my thoughts are with you. If you miss me as much as I miss you, we both miss each other terribly. Today I received five letters from you. Mail call is something that I always look forward to.

Darling, I'm glad to hear that the baby is doing so well and that she is as pretty as a picture. I am always thinking about what I will do when I first see her.

By this time you know how [well] we are making out here in France. If it keeps going our way, I know it won't be long before I come home. Darling, don't worry about me. I'll be all right

Darling, I haven't been able to contact Roger yet; in fact I haven't been anywhere near him since D-Day. His Battalion has always been quite a distance from me, but I hope to catch up with him soon.

For security reasons, no mail of any kind left England from May 10 through June 6.

I'm sorry that James is not feeling well. I hope he gets admitted to the hospital.

Glad you received the pictures. I don't think they are very good.

The blotches you see on this page are made by rain. I'm sitting in my foxhole, and the tent is covering the foxhole, but drops still come through.

Glad to hear that Fred likes the Navy. *[Fred served aboard the U.S.S General John Pope, a troop ship. He was not discharged until 1946.]* Honey, write to Fred as often as you can. A boy in the service wants more than anything else letters from his loved ones. You say you sent Fred candy, and you ask if I want anything. I don't care for candy, but I would like some jars of green peppers, hot peppers, Salami, and cheese. You know what I like.

Tell Lama that when I see her, I'm going to kiss her just like I did when I first met her at Ms. Whitten's. I won't care if her husband is watching.

You say you took some pictures with Mary Dean. I hope you will send me some. You saw the movie "Cover Girl"? I haven't seen that picture, and I don't know when I'll see another one. You say you saw three paratroopers in town? I hope my honey has eyes for only one paratrooper. As Li'l Abner would say, "Namely me."

Tell Sandra I said thank you for the sweet Father's Day Card. The new brown shoes don't look so good on her? I told you that nobody in the Bonilla family looks good in brown.

I have a great big mustache. I'll try to get a picture made and send it to you.

Darling, the American Red Cross is doing an excellent job here and in England.

Goodnight Darling, until I can write again. Give my love to the family.

Your Husband,

Nicky

July 1944

German V-I remote controlled rockets hit London killing and injuring thousands. In France, The U. S. First Army began a general offensive toward the east. Since D-Day, the Allies had landed 920,000 men in Normandy.

Stung by his failure to stop the invasion, Marshal Karl Von Rundstedt asked to be relieved of command of German forces in the west. Hitler put General Gunter von Kluge in command. Fierce fighting continued in Normandy. The R.A.F. bombed Caen in preparation for a final assault on the city. The United States recognized the government of the French Republic headed by General de Gaulle.

On July 20, a violent explosion shook the Wolf's Lair, Hitler's headquarters in a forest in East Prussia. Several of Hitler's staff were wounded or killed by a bomb placed in a meeting room. Hitler was unharmed. Minister of Propaganda Joseph Goebbles announced on Berlin radio that Hitler was saved by the will of the Almighty. The hunt for the leader of the assassination plot began. Claus Schenk von Stauffenberg had placed the bomb in Hitler's headquarters hoping to end the war and save the German people from more suffering. He flew to Berlin believing that Hitler was dead. In Berlin, Stauffenberg and approximately 500 other conspirators were executed. Many high-ranking officers, including Rommel, committed suicide.

Saturday
July 1, 1944
8:30 P.M.
Darling Opal,

I received your letters dated June 10 and June 12, and I was overjoyed. I am so sick of being away from you. I wish this war was over so I could come home to you and the baby. How is the baby? Don't you think the baby looks more like you than like me? You know I want her to have red hair just like yours. I haven't received the large picture of Sandra. I don't think I'll get it until I get to some rest area. Say Darling, are you still getting your war bonds every month and your family allotment?

Today the weather is bad. It has been raining all day, but I can always find a dry spot. I'm writing you from my foxhole. It's about six feet long, three feet deep, and four feet wide. I have a tent over the top. The sides of the hole are covered with some blankets we confiscated from the Germans. The bottom of the hole is covered with hay and a blanket doubled on top. We have three blankets over us, and two of us sleep in this hole.

From now on, my letters will be written in pencil. We can't get ink in France. If my letters are hard to read, blame the Germans. They did not leave any [ink when they left].

Darling, the night before D-Day, General Eisenhower spoke to me and asked me a few questions. Pictures were taken while he was speaking to me, so [a picture] might be in the newspapers or even in the newsreels. You might not recognize me because my face was blackened, but if you look [close] I know that you will recognize me.

Darling, I'm going to say goodnight. Give my love to the family, and always remember that I love you and adore you and I always will.

Goodnight.
Nicky

Sunday
July 2, 1944
10:30 P.M.
Dear Opal,

Today we were busy, and this is the first rest I've had all day, so I thought I would sit down and write you a few lines before it gets dark. It is too dangerous to write by candlelight.

Darling, I'm in the best of health, and I hope you are the same. It has been another rainy day. I sure hope [the rain] stops by tomorrow. I received three airmail letters, one V-mail, four newspapers, the large picture of Sandra and her baby shoes. Sandra is really beautiful.

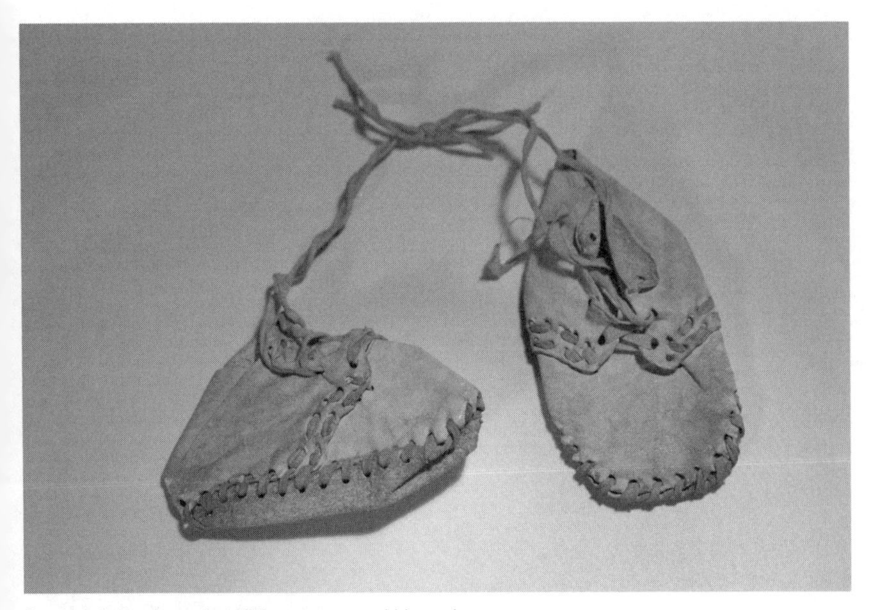

Sandra's baby shoes that Nicky wore around his neck.
Photo by Joe Loehle

By the time this letter reaches you, I should be in a rest area where I can bathe and shave every day and feel like a human being again.

I miss you and my daughter so much. I will always love you no matter how far away I am or how long I stay away.

Goodnight Darling, until tomorrow. I will try my best to write again. Give my love to the family.

Always yours,
Nicky

Leaving France

The Allies liberated Caen on July 9. In Normandy, 25 of 35 German Divisions were destroyed; 240,000 men were killed or wounded, and 200,000 were taken prisoner. The 101st suffered 4,000 casualties in a force of 13,500 men. Two hundred men of the 502nd were killed or died of wounds; six hundred were injured, and fifty were missing or captured. From June 29 until July 10, the 101st bivouacked in the Tollevast area. Men of the division had not assembled in one area since they left England. The division was relieved July 10; soldiers were transported to a bivouac area behind Utah Beach. There, troops loaded on to L.S.T. s, and on July 13, the L.S.T.s put in at Southampton, England.

Standing on a German pillbox, an elevated concrete gun emplacement, on July 7, General Maxwell Taylor had addressed the troops: "You hit the ground running toward the enemy. You have proved that the German soldier is no superman. You have beaten him on his own ground, and you can beat him on any ground." [18]

The men of the 101st had kept their rendezvous with destiny, and another rendezvous awaited them.

WESTERN UNION

Na358 INTL=SANS ORIGNE VIA WU CABLE 23 17 /355PLC
MRS NICHOLAS BONILLA
1920 3RD AVE SOUTH
IRONDALE ALA= FY BHAM FONE.

DARLING SAFE AND WELL. GOING ON FURLOUGH. NEED 125 DOLLARS IN A HURRY.
LOVE NICKY.

July 23, 1944
Hello, My Darling,

When you got my telegram asking for money, you knew I was in England. I returned from furlough, and I had thirteen letters from you, two from my mother, and one from Farris. I just now received the money order you sent, and I'm glad it came. I borrowed money, and now I can pay it back. I got the package you sent. The Salami went bad, but the cheese was good. I'm going to have some sardines when I finish this letter.

While I was on furlough, I went to the Red Cross and inquired about Roger Gray. He was wounded, but he'll be out of the hospital in a day or so. I'm sure Mary Dean has heard the good news.

After I checked on Richard, I rode the train all day to Scotland. I arrived about midnight and got a hotel room. I woke up about noon the next day, ate, dressed, and went to the movies. I saw Danny Kaye in "Up in arms," and Darling, that was the funniest picture I've seen in a long time. It was a scream.

I went to a tavern and drank a Scotch; I ate a steak, and I even drank a cup of tea. I went

Nicky in his Class A Uniform with new campaign medals. The photo was taken in England after D-Day.

back to the hotel and I spent a couple of hours in the Turkish bath. Then I went to bed, but my Darling, I couldn't sleep. I thought about how much I miss you and the baby, and I just tossed and turned. I ordered a bottle of Scotch and drank until I got sleepy. I woke up the next day with a terrible headache.

You know, two pretty girls were with me the whole time. I love these girls very much, and why shouldn't I? They are my wife and my daughter. We had a grand time, Sandra, you and I. We even went fishing.

You were with me in spirit, and you always will be. I'm going to read my letters before lights out. Tell Sandra that her daddy will be home soon.

Always yours,
Nicky

July 24, 1944
Dear Opal,

I did not receive mail today, but I don't mind because I'm still reading the letters I got yesterday. How is our charming daughter?

Honey, the food you sent is terrific, so good that I've eaten almost all of it. I ate sardine sandwiches, smoked herring sandwiches, caviar sandwiches, and anchovy sandwiches. I washed it down with English beer and ate some olives

Do you remember, when I first came to England, I said the weather was always bad? Well, now it is clear and cool. Here we wear our winter uniforms all year round.

I'm sending you some souvenirs. I got a few pairs of wooden shoes, a toy parachute for Farris, and some English, French, and German money. I'm glad to hear that Fred is home. Does he like the Navy, or is sorry he joined? Is James feeling better?

Darling, do you remember Pete Botzis? You met him in Fayetteville. He was killed in action in France. I hate that. He was a good boy.

Love always,
Nicky

★ ★ ★ ★ ★ ★ ★ ★ ★ ★ ★ ★ ★

Nicky sent Opal a copy of *Stars and Stripes* dated July 25. The newspaper reported on the Allied bombing of German positions in France and Italy.

EIGHTH AND R.A.F. BLAST GERMANY
[No byline]

American fighter planes ranged southwest Germany yesterday after a night in which the RAF hurled close to 3,000 tons of explosives on Kiel in the first major attack since D-Day on a great enemy industrial area and Mosquitoes dropped 4,000-pound block-busters on Berlin.

While 8th Air Force warplanes swept without opposition over the Reich, nearly 500 escorted heavy bombers flew from Italian bases in a widespread attack on enemy airdromes and a harbor in southern France and other objectives in northern Italy and southern Jugoslavia [sic].

Attacking German airfield and strafing transportation and communication facilities, 8th pursuits destroyed more than a dozen planes on the ground and shot three observation craft out of the air.

★ ★ ★ ★ ★ ★ ★ ★ ★ ★ ★ ★ ★

July 25, 1944
Hello Sweetheart,

Another day has passed, and I am another day closer to coming home. Nothing exciting going on here, just routine training.

Do you still love me and miss me? Does Sandra still look at my picture and say "Daddy"?

Remember Bing Crosby's song, "You Made Me Love You"? That is exactly what you did. We have had a lifetime of sweet romance, and now we have a darling baby. We are together, the three of us, and nothing can separate us, not even this war.

The wooden shoes that Nicky sent home as a souvenir. They are marked "Picked up in France June 12, 1944."
Photo by Joe Loehle

Today I finished eating the food you sent, and Honey, it was good. By the time you get this letter, Fred will be back at his base. I know he enjoyed being home.

A boy who sleeps next to me just asked me how to spell "miserable." That is one word I know how to spell.

I have only one heart,
and it is yours forever.
Nicky

July 26, 1944
Dear Opal,

Today I received your letters of July 16, 17, and 18. It was nice to hear from Farris. He is a smart boy. Give my love to all the family.

I'm sorry the telegram frightened you. Don't worry about me. I'll be fine. While I was on furlough, I stopped in London and bought myself a fountain pen, and it is giving me lots of trouble. Do you remember that I told you we bought a radio when we arrived in England? We have had good luck with it. I'm listening to it now as I write.

You ask me about writing at 10:30 P.M. while it is still light. In France and England during the summer, it doesn't get dark until midnight, and it gets light at about 5:00 A.M.

I miss both my darlings. I look forward to a day when I will sail into New York Harbor past the Statue of Liberty. I will see the Empire State Building getting closer and closer. When I get to the pier, I'll strain my eyes looking for you and Sandra. When I see you, I'll be in heaven.

Would you rather be surprised? You will be in Mom's house helping her cook or looking after Sandra. You will hear a knock on the door. You will come to the door, and I will be standing there. Which reunion do you prefer?

Love always,
Nicky

July 28, 1944
My Darling Nicky,

Hello, How are you tonight? Safe and well. I surely hope you are. I'm fine and Sandra is fine, too. I just got her to sleep. She didn't want to go to bed tonight. She would play all night if I would let her.

This afternoon we visited with Mary Dean. She got a cablegram from Roger and she was very glad to hear from him. She has been worried about him lately.

Darling, I'm anxious to receive some mail from you. I hope I get a letter tomorrow. I love you so much. I think of you all the time. I pray that it won't be much longer until the war is over and you can return to us.

All the folks are fine. They send their love. Take good care of my Nicky Boy, and write as often as you can.

I love you,

Opal

AUGUST 1944

In Amsterdam, the Gestapo captured Otto Frank and his family, including daughter Anne. Family members were sent to different concentration camps. Anne died at Bergen-Belsen in 1945, but Otto survived Auschwitz and published Anne's diary in 1977.

U.S.S.R. troops invaded Romania, and occupying German troops surrendered. Allies liberated Florence and the U.S. 3rd Army was formed under the command of General Patton. The Allies began landing in the South of France in Operation Anvil.

Although paratroopers of the 101st led the way in driving German armies from France, they missed the liberation of Paris. Hitler had ordered Paris burned, but General Dietrich von Choltitz disobeyed the order. He did not want to be known in history as the man who burned one of the most beautiful cities in Europe. The French Resistance attacked the German garrison, and on August 25, Allied troops marched into Paris. For the first time since September 1, 1939, Paris was once again the "City of Light."

Marshall Petain, head of the collaborationist Vichy government of France, fled to Switzerland after the Allied invasion, but when Paris was liberated, he returned to France. He was arrested and charged with treason. He was sentenced to death, but his sentence was commuted to life imprisonment. He died in prison in 1951.

In England, the 101st received replacements and new uniforms and equipment. The division held a memorial service for the men killed in France, and soon a series of alerts began. Troops were isolated, and they received combat equipment and ammunition. The 101st was to jump into France twenty-five miles southwest of Paris on August 19, but the drop was cancelled because of the rapid advance of General Patton's tank corps and other ground forces. A jump into Belgium near Lille, France, was also cancelled because of the success of the war on the ground.

The Red Ball Express, manned by African-American soldiers, drove 3,000 trucks over a 700-mile route, 24 hours a day, for 81 days, to supply the Allied advance with gasoline, ammunition, food, and medicine.

Chapter Seven

Operation Market Garden

SEPTEMBER 1944

The Allied sweep across Europe slowed, but Pisa in Itlay was liberated. General Patton's 3rd U.S. Army liberated Verdun in France as the British pushed toward Le Havre. Allies attacked three German garrison at Brest in Brittany, but the Nazis held. General Eisenhower's Army advanced toward the Ruhr, and General Patton's forces moved toward the Saar. Supplying the rapidly advancing armies became increasingly difficult. The Allies liberated Brussels on September 4; within a week, the Belgian government returned to the capital.

The first V-2 rockets fell in London on September 8. The missiles flew too fast to be intercepted by fighters and they were deadly. Allied bombers answered the attacks by bombing launch sites in northern France. On September 11, allies entered Germany. General Eisenhower decided to postpone an operation to liberate the port of Antwerp, and commanders made plans for the invasion of Holland. The First Allied Airborne Army, commanded by Lieutenant-General Lewis Brereton would invade Holland, secure important bridges, and open a road into the Ruhr, the industrial center of Germany.

In the U.S., canned goods, clothing and fabric, fats and oils, dairy products, gasoline, metal, and tires were rationed. Americans supported the war effort by buying war bonds, volunteering for the Red Cross, the United Services Organization, U.S.O., and civil defense jobs. They salvaged newspapers, rubber, aluminum, and tin.

★ ★ ★ ★ ★ ★ ★ ★ ★ ★ ★ ★ ★ ★

The following letters were returned to Opal in November 1944.

September 5, 1944
My Darling Nicky,

How are you tonight? We are well, and as Mom says, "Doing well is hard to beat." I am lonesome for you. Today, Sandra opened the icebox, and when I went to check on her, I found her eating a stick of butter. Then we went to the store for Mom. I bought several things including sharp cheddar cheese. I put the groceries in the carriage with Sandra. Before I noticed what she was doing, she got into the sack, took the cheese out, and she was eating the cheese, tin foil and all.

We went to the new post office. It's quite nice, and I like having a box. I can get my mail after 5:00 P.M. if I want to. Sometimes it's that late before I can get out of the house.

This time last year, you were on your way across and Sandra was born; two years ago, you were in New York, and we were just beginning to talk about getting married. Time brings many changes, doesn't it?

Next week, Sandra and I will go to town to have a large picture made for you. Mom will bake a birthday cake, and I'll take snapshots of Sandra with her cake.

Mom is sewing tonight. She is making a little dress for Sandra. Mom sews very well. She can see a picture in a newspaper or magazine and make a pattern for a dress just like in the picture. She can make the latest styles very economically. A ready-made dress costs five or six dollars. I learned to sew in school, but I haven't done needlework since then.

I hope it won't be long before you come home. Some people say the war will be over in six months. Even if it is only that long, Sandra will be a big girl when you see her.

Yours always,
Opal and Sandra

September 8, 1944
Darling Nicky,

I didn't get a chance to write yesterday. I was too busy taking care of Sandra and Patricia. Today they are playing with their dolls, chasing each other through the house, and jabbering. They'll get tired of that, and they will try to slip out the door to play in the yard . . . .

Aunt Hattie came to spend the day. She brought a chocolate pie. I told her I'd like to learn to make a pie that good for you. Dot and James are sleeping, and Dad is working in the garden. Unless we have company, Mom is always cleaning, cooking, and washing. At night, she pieces quilt tops while we listen to the radio.

Always yours,
Opal and Sandra

September 10, 1944
Darling Nicky,

I hope you are safe and well. Sandra is sleeping. It has been cold here. Dad made a fire, and it feels good. Pearl and Farris came out tonight and stayed a while. Pearl said to tell you hello . . . .

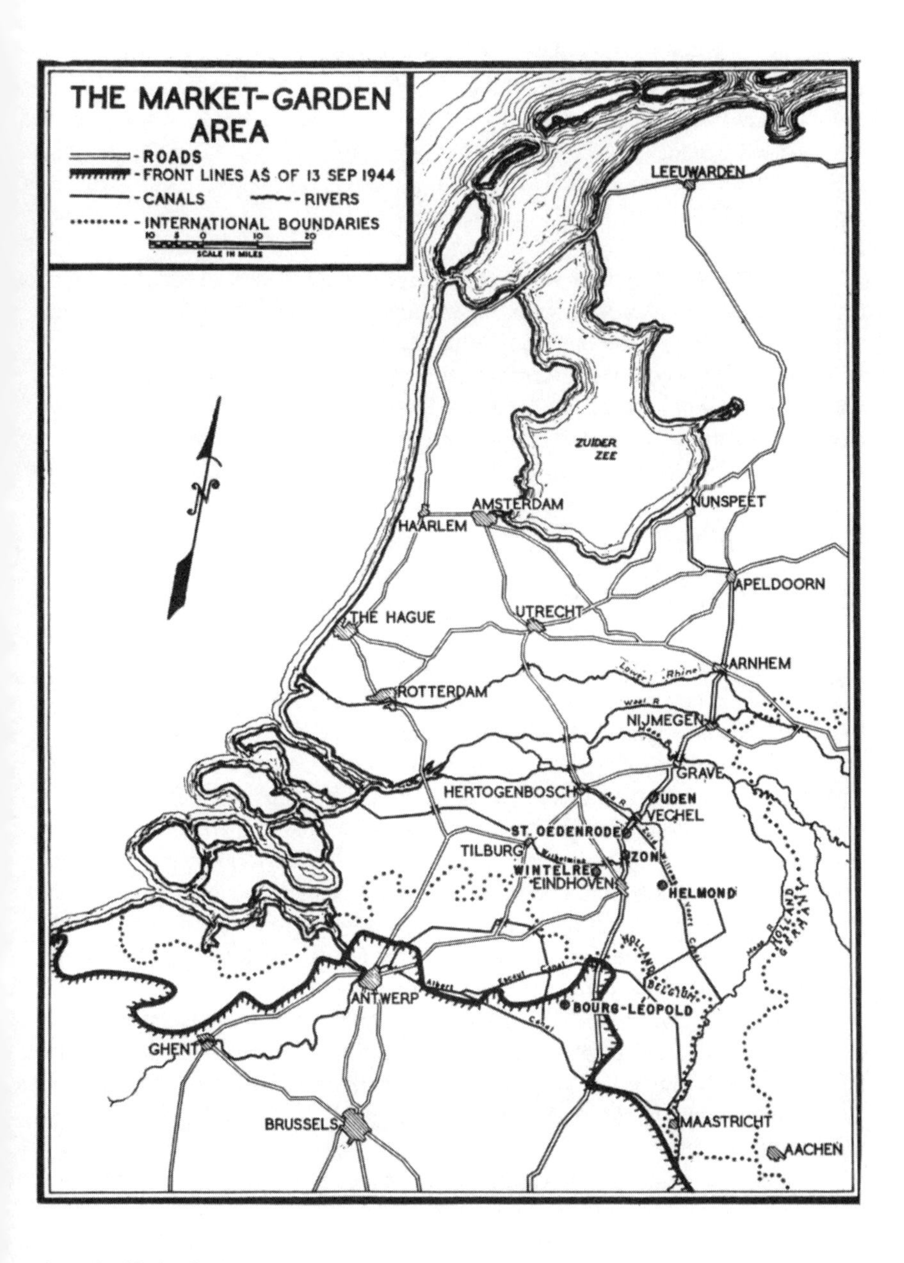

Operation Market Garden

When I ask Sandra how old she is, she holds up one little finger. Don't you think she's smart?

Yours always,

Opal and Sandra

September 10, 1944

Darling Nicky,

I didn't write last night, so I thought I'd drop a line before Dad goes to the post office. I am in the back yard with Sandra and Patricia. They are in the playpen, and they are crying to get out. They want to run around the yard like a couple of wild Indians. It is cool this morning, and Mom says we will have an early fall. Aunt Hattie, Mom's sister, and Aunt Ida, Mom's sister-in-law, visited. They love Sandra and Patricia. Everyone is thinking of you and praying for you.

I hope to get mail this morning. I haven't heard from you in a long time.

I love you with all my heart.

Opal and Sandra

Market Garden Plan

Field Marshal Montgomery wanted revenge for the British troops killed and captured when they could not be evacuated at Dunkirk; he wanted revenge for the Battle of Britain and the V-1 and V-2 rocket attacks on London; he wanted British troops to march into Berlin, and he wanted to be in command of those troops. Operation Market Garden was his plan, supported by General Eisenhower, for a narrow-front thrust into Holland using both ground and air operations.

Approximately 30,000 American, British, and Polish troopers were to parachute or ride gliders behind enemy lines into the Netherlands and capture eight bridges along a corridor from Eindhoven in the south to Arnhem in the north. Then, British tanks and infantry would cross the Rhine River and break the Siegfried Line, German defenses in the west.

General Eisenhower was to order General Patton to halt his advance across Europe and hold in place until after Operation Market Garden. Since much of the land was marsh-like with many rivers, canals, ditches, and dikes crossing the Dutch countryside, paratroopers had to secure roads and bridges before ground forces could advance.

Once they had landed, paratroopers would have limited firepower or mobility. Supply lines would become even longer.

German troops who had withdrawn from France (approximately, 15,000 men and 250 tanks), were gathered in Belgium and Holland. Dutch Resistance reported panzer units in Arnhem, but commanders ignored the reports. In a crashed glider on the first day of the invasion, German intelligence found top-secret plans for

Operation Market Garden

Operation Market Garden. The plans should never have left Allied headquarters.

★ ★ ★ ★ ★ ★ ★ ★ ★ ★ ★ ★ ★

```
WESTERN UNION

BM      NA      INTL   CD     SANS ORIGINE
VIA     WU     CABLE 17      SEPT 10
NLT
MRS NICHOLAS BONILLA
1920 3RD AVE SOUTH
IRONDALE ALA

DEAR OPAL
WITH A TEAR EVERY YEAR I WILL REMEMBER MY DAUGHTER'S
BIRTHDAY.
NICHOLAS L. BONILLA.    11 15 A M

WESTERN UNION

BM      Na      INTL   CD     SANS ORIGINE
VIA     WU      CABLE 18 SEPT 10 NTL

MRS NICHOLAS L BONILLA
1920 3RD AVE SOUTH
IRONDALE ALA

I LOVE YOU. I LOVE YOU.

NICHOLAS BONILLA.                1115 AM
```

September 12, 1944
My Darling Nicky,

How is the most wonderful husband and father in this world? You are always thoughtful; I knew you wouldn't forget Sandra's birthday. Thank you for sending the telegrams. I'm relieved to know that you are well.

I am sitting at the kitchen table writing, and Sandra is sitting in her highchair across from me. She has a piece of paper and a pencil. She is writing a letter to her daddy. You should see how well she can hold that pencil. Sandra is unusually smart to be so young. Everyone says so.

Now a train is passing, and Sandra is yelling at the train. When we are outside and we see a train coming, Sandra waves at the engineer and the man in the caboose.

Tomorrow on her birthday, I am going to take Sandra to town and have her picture made. Then I'll make a roll of pictures here at the house . . . .

I love you with all my heart.

Opal and Sandra

September 13, 1944

My Darling Nicky,

Sandra's birthday was grand. If you had been here, it would have been perfect. Mom made a white cake with a pink candle. Sandra looked pretty in her little blue dress with white lace and new white socks and white shoes. I did not take Sandra to town to have her picture made because one of our friends came to spend the day. Mom was busy and Dot was sleeping, so I couldn't leave. After our friend left, I took Sandra and Patricia to the drug store and bought them ice cream; then we visited Mary Dean and Scarlett.

Our family and friends gave Sandra nice gifts: money, three dresses, socks, a sweater, and a slip. I know Pearl will bring a gift when she comes to visit on Sunday.

When Sandra woke up this morning, she said, "Ice." I don't know if she meant the icing on the cake or ice cream. I let Sandra and Patricia eat the cake with their hands, and they just tore it apart. When they were finished, that cake looked awful, and their faces were covered with icing.

Sandra kisses your picture every morning and every night, and she says "Oh, Daddy." Sandra got the picture of you in your jump suit, the one I keep on the vanity, and she broke it. I was afraid she had gotten glass in her hands, but she didn't. Sometimes she is a bad little girl. I am sending you the candle from Sandra's cake.

Sandra Bonilla and Scarlett Gray in Sandra's carriage on the main street of Irondale. The Irondale Café is behind Scarlett., May 1944.

Fred wrote. He is in good health, but he is lonely. He misses the family and the boys that he has known all his life. I am lonely too, and I will be lonely until you come home.

Yours always,
Opal and Sandra

September 14, 1944
My Darling Nicky,

Darling, tomorrow is the first day for mailing Christmas presents. I hate to think that you'll be away for another Christmas. If only I knew what you wanted. I'm going to send you food, razorblades, soap, etc. If you need anything else, let me know. All I want is to have you back home. That would be the greatest Christmas gift I could get.

We got a letter from Fred. He hopes to come home for a few days soon. Dot and Dad are working. James has been feeling better, and he is working too. Mom works hard taking care of all of us. Good night for now.

Remember, we love you.
Opal and Sandra

September 15, 1944
My Darling Nicky,

When I am out of her sight, Sandra calls me, "Mom, Mom, Mom." Today I left the door open, and Sandra and Patricia slipped out into the yard. When I found them, they were going to Mrs. Massey's next door. . . .

Yours always,
Opal and Sandra

September 17, 1944

The R.A.F. destroyed German fighters on the ground, taking most of the Luftwaffe out of action for the invasion of Holland. In mid-morning, the 101st Airborne Division boarded C-47s and began leaving airfields in England. Operation Market Garden involved the greatest collection of aircraft ever assembled: 5,000 fighters, bombers, and transports, and 2,500 gliders. Forces included 20,000 soldiers, 500 vehicles, some 300 artillery pieces, and 590 tons of equipment. As planes thundered above, English men, women, and children cheered and waved. Tank columns of the British Second Army were poised on the Dutch/Belgium border.

The 101st was to drop into Holland north of Eindhoven and to capture and hold the highway from Eindhoven through Zon [Son]. The road would become known as "Hell's Highway." The 101st was also to take Veghel, Zon, and Eindhoven, and their bridges. The 82nd Airborne Division was to take towns and bridges from Grave to Nijmegen and the Grosbeek Heights. The 1st British

A paratrooper jumps into Holland during Market Garden and lands near a haystack.

Airborne Division and 1st Polish Parachute Regiment were to secure the high ground near Arnhem. Then British XXX Corps, with Guards Armoured leading, would drive across the secured bridges into Germany.

Despite thick smoke and bursts of flak, pilots held their courses, and troopers jumped as scheduled, even as planes exploded in mid-air. Six C-47s were shot down. The 101st made a perfect drop; General Maxwell Taylor jumped with the 502nd into the area near Zon. Dutch civilians greeted Allied troops with cheers, waves, handshakes, and food, beer, and wine. They unfurled the flags of the Netherlands that they had hidden from occupying German forces

The 501st, commanded by Col. Howard R. Johnson took Veghel and its bridges. The 502nd, commanded by Lt. Col. John H. Michaelis was held in reserve near Zon with the task of serving as a connection between the 501st to the north and the 506th in the South. 1st Battalion of the 502nd, led by Lt. Col. Patrick Cassidy, seized St. Oedenrode and nearby bridges. Col. Robert Sink's 506th took Zon, but Nazis blew the bridge.

General Taylor believed that capturing the bridges over the Wilhelmina Canal at Best was vital. Since the bridge at Best was a secondary objective, thought to be lightly defended, Lt. Col. Michaelis sent Lt. Edward L. Wierzbowski's platoon to capture the bridge; then H Company of the 502nd, led by Capt. Robert E. Jones, joined the battle. Soon all of 3rd Battalion commanded by Lt. Col. Robert

G. Cole was fighting near Best. Through marshes, along canals and dikes, the battalion fought against overwhelming numbers of German soldiers. Darkness fell and the battalion dug in.

Meanwhile, British paratroopers occupied houses at the north end of the road bridge at Arnhem. The railroad bridge was blown. The Brits found that their radios were not working properly, and it was impossible to co-ordinate their attack with that of the ground forces.

Hitler gave Operation Market Garden absolute priority. Crushing the attack in Holland was more critical than defending the Fatherland. German commanders sent trainloads of infantry and supplies into the battle. At dusk, a fine, quiet rain began to fall. By midnight, German armored cars were defending the south end of the Arnhem Bridge. Rain fell all night.

September 18, 1944

A pea-soup fog and heavy afternoon and evening rain delayed departures of planes and gliders in England, Belgium, and northern France. Only 97 Royal Air Force sorties were flown, while 190 Luftwaffe fighters provided air support to meet the Allied attack.

When planes were able to take off, 91 out of 904 gliders were lost, and 11 of 117 Liberator resupply planes were lost. Of the gasoline, ammunition, food, and water dropped near Best, Allied troops recovered only one-half. German soldiers got the rest. British tanks advanced 20 miles, reaching American paratroopers near the bridge at Grave. The operation fell behind schedule. German antitank guns disabled British tanks and wreckage blocked the highway.

The 506th occupied Eindhoven and secured its bridges. British engineers began construction of a temporary steel bridge across the Zon.

German and American troops poured into the fields and forests around Best. Patrick Cassidy's 1st Battalion of the 502nd defended St. Oedenrode. The 2nd Battalion of 502nd, commanded by Lt. Col. Steve Chappuis, joined the bitter fight. Defending the area was the German Fifteenth Army. The 502nd attacked across open fields without adequate supporting fire.

Col. S.L.A. Marshall in *Men Against Fire* wrote that the advance of D Company, [Nicky's company] was unique in military history for "achieving almost perfect order in infantry maneuver under modern conditions of fire." He described the advance as follows:

> The Dutch had been haying and the fields ahead were full of small piles of uncollected hay. That was the only concealment. From left to right the line rippled forward in perfect order and with perfect discipline each group of two or three dashing to the next hay pile as it came their turn. It was as if the piles were of concrete. But machine-gun fire cut into them, sometimes setting the hay afire, sometimes wounding or killing the men behind them. That did not stop anyone except the dead and wounded. [18]

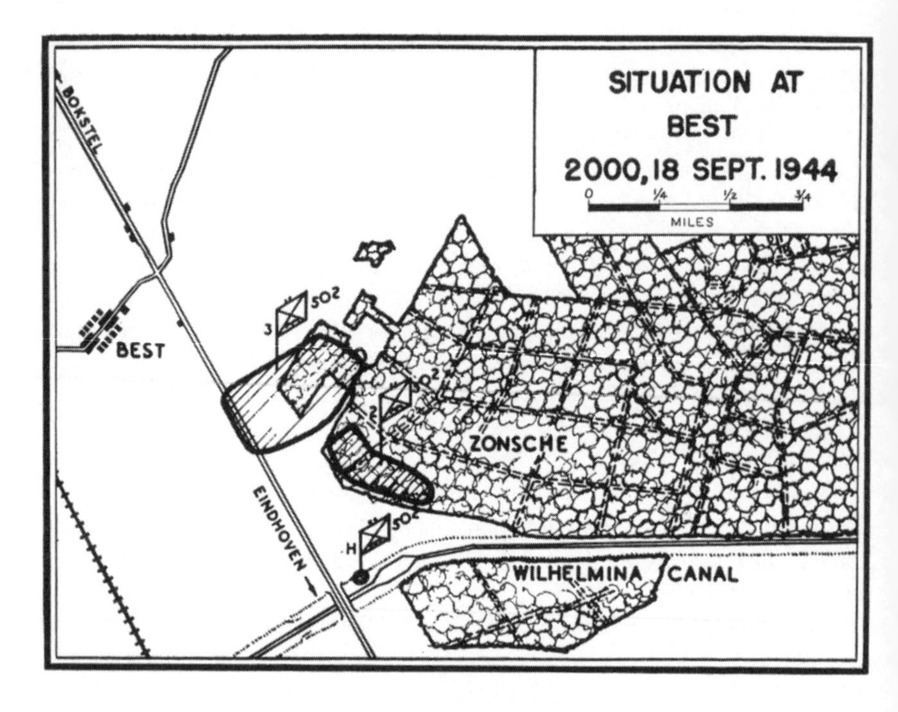

Battle at Best

The battle raged around 2nd and 3rd Battalions. The September 18 entry in the Journal of the Third Battalion, 502 PIR, reads, "Enemy closing in, situation getting desperate." Afternoon flights brought reinforcements including the 327th Glider Infantry. However, the 502nd failed to take the bridge, and it was blown.

Lt. Col. Cole, awarded the Medal of Honor for heroic actions in France, was killed by a sniper's bullet. Major John P. Stopka took command of 3rd Battalion of the 502nd.

Pfc. Joe E. Mann, Company H, 502nd

As Nazi infantry reinforcements streamed into Best on September 18, Pfc. Joe Mann fired bazooka shots into a German ammunition dump and destroyed it. Mann was hit twice by rifle fire. Later in the afternoon, Mann was hit by two more bullets. After he was bandaged, he begged Lt. Wierzbowski to allow him to remain in a foxhole with defenders rather than go to a safer area with other wounded. At first light on September 19, Nazis attacked Wierzbowski's position and threw five grenades at the foxhole. One went wild; three were thrown out before they could explode, but one exploded in the face of Pvt. Vincent Laino, blinding him. Even blinded, Laino was able to throw another grenade from the foxhole. For his bravery, he was awarded the Silver Star. Mann was sitting against the back of the trench when the next grenade hit. He felt it land behind him, and because his wounded arms were useless, he yelled, "Grenade!" and fell back covering the explosion with his own body. He said, "My back's gone," and he died within minutes. [19]

For his sacrifice, he was awarded the Medal of Honor.

★★★★★★★★★★★★★

Sept 18, 1944
My Darling Nicky,

Sorry I didn't write Saturday or yesterday, but Mom was away, Dot was working, and I had to keep Sandra and Patricia by myself. With two of them to look after, I can't do anything else.

Leaves on the trees around the house are turning yellow and red. Mom's pansies are blooming. They flourish in cool weather. Mom says pansies look like little monkey faces. Dad is planting onions, kale, and turnips in his little garden. I see children walking down the sidewalk wearing new school clothes and carrying book satchels. Soon I'll be shopping for your Christmas gifts. Darling, I wish I knew what to send. Let me know what you'd like . . . .

Yours always
Opal and Sandra

September 19, 1944

Fog and rain in England delayed departure of the third wave of airborne troops and supplies. The 1st Polish Parachute Brigade was eager to join the fight, but the scheduled jump was cancelled. When planes were finally able to fly, 43 Allied aircraft and 385 gliders took off, but 189 were forced to turn back or were shot down.

Allied planes strafed the area, and German fire decreased. The 82nd captured the bridge at Nijmegen. The 501st established outposts at Erde and in the Heeswijk-Dinter area. The 506th took Eindhoven and marched toward Zon where fighting continued. Nazis attacked defenders of St. Oedenrode.

By afternoon, almost the entire 502nd was fighting against fierce opposition near Best. The bridge was blown, but British tanks rumbled to the front and, with their support and reinforcements, the 502nd won the battle. They destroyed a force of 2,000 to 3,000 Nazis. Some German soldiers trying to surrender were killed by their comrades. Lt. Col. Michaelis was wounded and command of the regiment passed to Lt. Col. Steve Chappius.

Along the road to Schijndel, German defenders who threatened to flank the battalion blocked the 1st Battalion of the 502nd. Sgt. James McCrory of the Irish Guards had dropped out of the British tank action when his vehicle was damaged and could travel only five miles an hour. McCrory joined the attack of the 502nd and knocked out three 20mm guns.

When the most bitter fighting had ended, Staff Sergeant Charles Dohun of the 502nd went in search of his captain, LeGrand Johnson. Dohun found Johnson badly wounded, but alive. Dohun placed Johnson and four other wounded men in a Jeep and drove toward the hospital at Zon. Dohun had to hide from a German patrol, and when he reached the hospital, he found long lines of soldiers waiting for treatment. Fearing his Captain would die, Douhan appealed to a surgeon for help. When the surgeon told Douhan that his Captain would have to wait, Douhan pulled his .45 and threatened to shoot the surgeon. The surgeon treated Johnson. When Dohun returned to 2nd Battalion, Lt. Col. Steve Chappuis told Dohun that he had committed a court-martial offense. Chappius had Dohun arrested—for one minute—and Dohun returned to his unit.

The Allies ran out of medical supplies. At Arnhem Bridge, British paratroopers, short of food, water, and ammunition, were receiving fire from Nazi 100-mm guns. Tanks and mortars pounded the Brits, but Lt. Col. John Frost and his men refused to surrender.

At dusk, the Luftwaffe bombed and strafed Eindhoven, killing 250 civilians, wounding 800, and leaving much of the city in flames.

Opal read the news of the attack in the September 19 *Birmingham News*.

> REINFORCED ALLIES DRIVE ON, IMPERIL [WAAL] FLANK, SURGE EASTWARD TOWARD GERMANY . . . .
> Battle of Rhine on; Sky Troops Pour into Holland; Dutch Rail Hub Seized
>
> By James M. Long, London—AP—A powerful, growing army of Allied sky troops which vaulted [into] Holland battled around the flank of the Siegfried line . . . .
>
> The airborne army descended in the area of Nijmegen and Arnhem, near the Reich and astride the two lower branches of the Rhine as well as near Eindhoven . . . . British ground forces were reported already 12 miles north of Eindhoven or halfway to Nijmegen and Arnhem . . . .

★ ★ ★ ★ ★ ★ ★ ★ ★ ★ ★ ★ ★

September 19, 1944
My Darling Nicky,

Hello Darling, How are you tonight? Sandra and Patricia are asleep. They have been into everything today, hiding under the beds and in the closets, climbing on top of the kitchen table.

Darling, Sandra has another tooth. That makes five. She is so cute with her big teeth. Gee! Can she bite. I tell her, "You're just like your dad, always trying to bite me."

I have read several stories about the invasion in the newspapers, and I have many new pictures of paratroopers for our scrapbook. I hope I hear from you soon. The last letter I received was dated July 28.

Our cousin Donald George came home. He was in England for eighteen months. Darling, I don't know much news to write, but I do know this—I love you and I always will.

Yours forever,

Opal and Sandra

September 20, 1944

Fog and rain in England continued to delay flights with reinforcements including glider troopers of the 82nd Airborne and 1st Polish paratroopers. North of Eindhoven along Hell's Highway, German tanks hit the 101st at dawn, but with the help of British armor, the Americans held their ground. Supplies were short; paradrops provided only one meal for troops, and no gasoline. At Arnhem, Nazi tanks pounded the houses where the British Red Devils were dug in, destroying the buildings one by one. The Brits ran out of food and water. No relief came, and Germans and the British arranged a brief truce to care for approximately 300 wounded. Col. John Frost was wounded by a mortar blast and taken prisoner. Dutch civilians were ordered to evacuate the battle zone, and the Luftwaffe continued to bomb Eindhoven.

In the *Birmingham News*, Opal read about the battles.

> BRITISH ARMOR AND SKY TROOPS LOCK IN BATTLE AT RHINE BRIDGEHEAD
> British Tanks across River, Dutch Assert
>
> By James E. Long—London —AP—British armor and Allied air-borne troops battled Wednesday night for crossings on the Lower Rhine in Holland with one foot in the door to the great Ruhr Valley of Germany and its war plants. Netherlands radio declared Wednesday night that British tanks have crossed the Lower Rhine at Nijmegen in Holland and are hitting northward toward Arnhem and the upper branch of the river.
>
> The U. S. First Army held onto its breaches in the Siegfried line despite heavy tank and infantry attacks by desperate Germans . . . .

★ ★ ★ ★ ★ ★ ★ ★ ★ ★ ★ ★ ★

September 20, 1944

My Darling Nicky,

How are you tonight? I hope you are safe and well. I am lonesome and blue. I want to see my husband.

Sandra has been asleep for about three hours. She goes to sleep a little earlier now, and most of the time she sleeps all night. Her days are busy. She and Patricia play from the minute they wake up until the minute they go to sleep.

Darling, Sandra's hair is still quite short, but it's beginning to curl, just like yours. Her eyes are turning hazel and they are beautiful. Darling, don't make me wait too long to hear from you. If you can't write, please send a telegram.

I am packing things to send you for Christmas. I hope you will like what I got. The last day to send packages is October 15. What do you want? Please let me know soon.

Our radio is broken, and I haven't heard music in a month now. When I read the newspapers, I see that the paratroopers are very busy. They are doing a fine job. I know you are working very hard. I can never tell you how proud I am. Good night, my Darling. Please take care of yourself.

Always yours,
Opal and Sandra

September 21, 1944

Biting cold weather with rain and fog again delayed resupply flights departing from England. At Arnhem Bridge, survivors of the British 1st Airborne Battalion ran out of ammunition or were overwhelmed. Some continued to fight with knives. They fought for 48 hours, for 12 hours without food and water. Of 10,005 men in the British 1st Division, only 2,163 were evacuated from Arnhem. Some 1,500 were killed and 6, 500 were taken prisoner.

In the early evening, the 1st Polish Parachute Regiment jumped into a hail of antiaircraft fire near Driel, but they were too late and too far away to help the men at Arnhem.

Soldiers of the 101st held on along "Hell's Highway" north of Eindhoven. The 502nd continued fighting near Best and St. Oedenrode, cleaning out pockets of German resistance. Troopers got their first supplies in four days. Of 117 Liberator resupply planes, 11 were lost.

Opal read about the desperate fighting in Holland in the September 21 *Birmingham Post*.

> AIRBORNE UNITS HELD IN CIRCLE;
> Fight for Strategic Span Is Waged By British at [Wall] Rhine
>
> By Howard Cowan,
> SUPREME HEADQUARTERS ALLIED EXPEDITIONARY FORCE,
> Sept. 21 (Thursday)—AP—British Second Army troops fought desperately Thursday to cross the Rhine River at Nijmegen, Holland in a race to rescue a huge pocket of Allied airborne forces isolated in the Arnhem sector and under slashing German attack.
>
> The all-important concrete bridge, a mile and a half long and 600 feet above the swift flowing Wall [Waal] Rhine, still is intact, headquarters declared officially at midnight, but it was held firmly by Germans, and a

great swirling battle was raging.

The airborne troops in the Arnhem sector were "completely surrounded" by the Nazis, headquarters said officially, and battled furiously in the pocket against the German ring . . . .

The great battle across the Rhine Delta, the German radio said, might prove a decisive Western Front engagement.

★ ★ ★ ★ ★ ★ ★ ★ ★ ★ ★ ★ ★

September 21, 1944
My Darling Nicky,

How are you tonight? Are you taking good care of yourself? I surely hope you are. Sandra went to sleep at 5 o'clock, and slept until 8 o'clock. Now she wants to stay up and play. Sandra has five teeth, and I think she will have two more in a few days.

Sandra can't be still for a minute. She plays with the pots and pans in the kitchen cabinets and takes the silverware out of the drawers. Right now, she is climbing on a chair trying to help me write. She was standing on a chair, and she fell. That really scared me. I try to watch her at all times. . . .

We received a letter from Fred today. He said he is graduating from Basic Engineering School, and he might have to ship out soon. He hopes he can come home for a few days. I know Fred will be a good sailor.

I love you with all my heart.

Opal and Sandra

September 22, 1944

Along Hell's Highway, German troops broke through an undefended section of road between Uden and Grave. Using almost half its strength, the 101st repelled the attack, hanging on to Veghel, but the road north to Arnhem was closed. Early in the morning, several rounds in an Allied pre-attack barrage fell short, landing on men of 502nd, C Company and causing eight casualties. Fighting raged from Veghel to Osterbeek, with the 101st forming a front in the Oedenrode-Veghel area. The Luftwaffe bombed and strafed Arnhem and Nijmegen. Weather prevented Allied planes taking off to fly resupply missions.

The Birmingham News reported that German troops had halted the Allied advance along Hell's Highway.

NAZIS STOP SKY TROOPS TRYING TO SAVE AIRBORNE FORCES
Situation Of Sky Troops Now Critical; Desperate Battle Is On; Tank Fight Raging

New York—AP—Airborne British and Poles, fiercely beset by a German counter attack from all sides, fought a desperate battle . . . to hold open the strategic crossing of the Rhine's upper branch in Holland so the Allies could sweep into Northern Germany.

The position of the airborne soldiers who leaped into the middle of the Germans northern river defenses 50 miles ahead of Allied lines Sunday night was officially described as critical at General Dwight D. Eisenhower's supreme headquarters.

★ ★ ★ ★ ★ ★ ★ ★ ★ ★ ★ ★ ★

The Allies abandoned the Market Garden plan on September 22, but fighting continued. The British at Arnhem held on grimly, but no relief came. General Eisenhower ordered a security blackout on news about all operations in Holland, and no official reports were given. Radio broadcasts from Berlin said that the Allied advance into Germany would be measured in inches and cost streams of blood. The 101st fought in Holland until November 27 suffering twice as many casualties afterward as in Operation Market Garden itself.

The greatest airborne operation in history ended in failure. A plan for invasion spread over several days, bad weather, poor intelligence, and communications breakdowns doomed the attack. Field Marshal Montgomery said that the operation was 90 percent successful because all objectives but Arnhem were taken, but without Arnhem, the other objectives meant nothing. Troopers fought with courage, and many men died for a length of highway leading nowhere. As Market Garden ended, the battle to liberate the port of Antwerp began.

Holland was occupied by thousands of German soldiers who needed equipment and food, but the Dutch government in exile called a railway strike, and civilian trains would transport neither military nor civilian supplies.

Nazis were furious, and reprisals were harsh. Rations were cut from 1,500 calories a day to 500: two slices of bread, two small potatoes, and half a sugar beet. Thus began the "Hunger Winter." Many Dutch civilians fell ill and died, many were transported to concentration camps, and many were killed—approximately 237,000.

Although Opal knew only what she read in newspapers, she learned later that on September 22, 1944, the day the Allies had abandoned Operation Market Garden, Nicky was killed. Letters Opal had written from September 5 through October 5 were returned. On each envelope, the word "Deceased" was written and the word "Verified" was stamped.

September 24, 1944
Dearest Nicky,

I haven't written in the past two nights because we've have had so much company. Pearl and Farris just left. They think of you and hope you will be home soon.

We got our radio fixed, and it is nice to hear music again.

Please forgive me, Darling, for not writing. I love you so much, and I've been thinking about you more than ever today. I dreamed about you last night. You were home. It was a warm, bright day, and the sun was shining on Sandra's hair. You and Sandra were running, playing and laughing. You were as happy together as a father and daughter could be. Oh! How I wish that dream would come true. Do you think it will? Darling, I pray night and day for your safe return.

Always yours,
Opal and Sandra

[On September 26, six thousand Allied survivors of Operation Market Garden were taken as P.O.W.s]

October 1, 1944
My Darling Nicky,

How are you Sweetheart? Are you safe and well? I pray that you are. Pearl and Farris came to visit. Patricia and Sandra love playing with Farris. He rides them around in the carriage and plays ball with them. Yesterday morning the little Negro boy Boots, the washwoman's grandson, came and tended to Patricia and Sandra. They like him, and he takes good care of them.

Someone told James that goat's milk would be good for his stomach, so he got a goat. Sandra and Patricia are fascinated with it.

We were expecting Fred, but he did not get to come home. We were very disappointed.

I've already mailed two packages for your Christmas, and I'll mail more next week. I wish I knew what you would like. I'll just take a chance and try to guess. Pearl and Farris wanted me to go home with them for a few days, but I told Pearl I could not go. Just why do you think I wouldn't go, Darling? Well, I am hoping that in the morning I will get a letter from my Darling Nicky Boy. I am very anxious. If only I could see you and tell you how much I love you.

Yours always,
Opal and Sandra

October 2, 1944
My Darling Nicky,

Hello Sweetheart, how are you? I hope you are safe and well. I received the package with the wooden shoes and the little parachute. I know Farris will like the chute.

Mary Dean visited this afternoon. She got two cards from Roger. He is fine. I think he has been in England for the past few months.

Darling, I love you so very much, and I miss you more than I can say. I don't think I can wait one more day to hear from you. I'll just imagine how grand it will be when you come home and see Sandra for the first time. I know she'll love her dad.

Always yours,
Opal and Sandra

October 3, 1944
Dearest Nicky,

How are you? Safe and well? Sandra and I went to the post office today, and I was praying I would get a letter from you, but I did not. I got a letter from Lama. She is still in Gadsden with her husband. She said she lost her temper at work and quit. She is thinking about going to Atlanta to look for a job.

Darling, I'm terribly anxious to hear from you. I miss you and think of you constantly. I want you to come home more than I have ever wanted anything. Goodnight for now.

Yours always,
Opal and Sandra

October 4, 1944
My Darling Nicky,

I went to town to buy more things for your Christmas. I didn't know what to get. I've sent two packages, and I'm sending four more—mostly food. I hope you enjoy it.

Mom kept Sandra while I was gone. Mom said she was good, but she got a bottle of ink, and she smeared it all over her dress, shoes, and socks. It was a mess! Her hands were covered with ink, and she put her hands in her mouth and smeared ink all over her face. That's what I saw when I walked in the door.

Sandra was so happy to see me that I couldn't be mad. She wanted me to hold her and kiss her, but Mom and I had to clean her up first. Sandra has seven teeth now . . . .

Darling, I pray night and day that you are safe. I want you to come home more than I have ever wanted anything.

Goodnight for now,
Opal and Sandra

October 5, 1944
My Darling Nicky,

I pray to God that you are safe and well. This morning and this afternoon, I've been working. Dad and I are planting grass. We're making the lawn behind the house bigger so Sandra and Patricia will have more room to play. Mom will plant more trees and flowers. She gets bulbs, seeds, and cuttings from her brothers and sisters, and friends and neighbors. Before long, the yard will look nice.

Darling, did I tell you I bought a new black hat? Bet you'll like this one. I hope it won't be long before I'll be getting dressed to meet you at the train station.

I cook dinner almost every Sunday while Mom is at church. Pearl and Farris usually come to visit, and they say I'm going to be a good cook. I want my husband to be proud of me.

We got a letter from Fred. He says Navy food is too good. He has gained from 152 pounds to 178. He is six feet tall, so he is a big boy.

Darling, Mom made Sandra three new dresses. Sandra loves new clothes. Mom laughs when Sandra makes a fuss about them. Sandra says, "Oh! Oh!" She wants to wear the dresses before Mom can finish sewing. Patricia sees them and says, "Mine," so Mom stays busy sewing for her granddaughters.

Darling, I'll say goodnight for now. I hope I get a letter from you tomorrow. I love you with all my heart and soul.

Yours always,
Opal and Sandra

October 6, 1944

In the little railroad depot in Irondale, the printer of the Teletype machine clattered as a telegram arrived:

WESTERN UNION

MRS NICHOLAS L BONILLA
1920 THIRD AVENUE SOUTH
IRONDALE ALABAMA

=THE SECRETARY OF WAR DESIRES ME TO EXPRESS HIS DEEP REGRET THAT YOUR HUSBAND PFC NICHOLAS L BONILLA WAS KILLED IN ACTION IN HOLLAND 22 SEPT 44. CONFIRMING LETTER FOLLOWS=
J A ULIO THE ADJUTANT GENERAL
1944

Nicky's wallet contains a lock of Sandra's hair.
Photo by Joe Loehle

The clerk in the telegraph office came to the Keith home to deliver the news to Opal.

Soon Nicky's personal effects were returned—a black plastic crucifix on a silver chain, a wallet containing pictures of Opal and Sandra, a lock of Sandra's hair, Sandra's baby shoes, the ribbon for the 502nd Unit Citation, and the silver parachute wings that Nicky had worn with pride.

Letters of Sympathy

October 11, 1944
My Dear Opal,

The death of your husband touched me deeply. I can sympathize with you because I understand what it is to lose one whom you loved so much. I pray that God will give you strength and you will find comfort in your baby. Hoping to see you soon, I am,

With love,
Mrs. H. R. Romeo

★ ★ ★ ★ ★ ★ ★ ★ ★ ★ ★ ★ ★

The Office of the Chief of Staff General George C. Marshall sent a formal card postmarked October 17, 1944.

"General Marshall extends his deepest sympathy in your bereavement. Your husband fought gallantly in a supreme hour of his country's need. His memory will live in the grateful heart of our nation."

★ ★ ★ ★ ★ ★ ★ ★ ★ ★ ★ ★ ★

United States Senator from Alabama, John Bankhead, sent the following letter:

November 30, 1944
Dear Mrs. Bonilla:

I have just learned with genuine regret that your husband was killed in action in the European area while nobly doing his part to help preserve our freedom. May I extend to you my sincere sympathy in your grief.

Sincerely yours,
John Bankhead

★ ★ ★ ★ ★ ★ ★ ★ ★ ★ ★ ★

The Secretary of War, Henry L Stimson, sent a letter:

December 7, 1944
My Dear Mrs. Bonilla:

At the request of the President, I write to inform you that the Purple Heart has been awarded posthumously to your husband, Private First Class Nicholas L. Bonilla who sacrificed his life in the defense of his country.

Little that we can do or say will console you for the death of your loved one. We appreciate the greatness of your loss, for in a very real sense, the loss suffered by any of us in the battle for our country is a loss shared by all of us. [With] the medal . . . goes my sincerest sympathy.

Sincerely yours,
Henry L Stimson

★ ★ ★ ★ ★ ★ ★ ★ ★ ★ ★ ★

The Catholic Chaplain of the 502nd, Father Joseph Andrejewski, sent two letters:

December 13, 1944
Re: Bonilla, Nicholas, PFC. 6877454
D Co, 2 Bn, 502nd Prcht Inf
Dear Mrs. Bonilla,

It is with personal deep sympathy that I extend to you my heartfelt condolence on the sad occasion of the loss of your husband, Nicholas, who has given his life in defense of his country's honor. We who revere Nicholas's heroism cannot doubt that God welcomes him with love.

Undoubtedly, you will find some consolation in the knowledge of the circumstances and particulars of how your husband was killed in action.

Nicholas made a successful jump into Holland, and immediately joined his unit in an attack against the enemy. From the time of the landing until Sept. 22, 1944, he fought with the courage and tenacity known of the Paratroopers, inflicting great losses on the enemy. Unfortunately, while attacking a fortified position held by the Germans on Sept. 22, Nicholas was instantly killed by an ENEMY automatic weapon. [The capitalization of the word "enemy" may be a response to the fact that some soldiers in the 504th had been killed by Allied fire.] He was buried with full military honors by a United States Army Chaplain of his own Faith. For information of the grave location, I must advise you to write to the Quartermaster General, ASF, Washington, DC. On the field [of] battle, Nicholas was an inspiration to his comrades.

With a humble prayer for the repose of his soul, and God's blessings on you, I remain,

Respectfully,
Joseph A. Andrejewski, Capt.
Catholic Chaplain.

December 15, 1944
Dear Mrs. Bonilla,

I am in receipt of your letter dated November 8, 1944, and accordingly have fulfilled your wishes by seeing to it that the packages received in your late husband's name will be distributed among the men of his outfit. Incidentally, about a week ago, I sent a formal letter through Army channels to you with all details of his death.

Again, I repeat my heartfelt sympathies to you and hope you will find solace in the knowledge that Nicholas did not sacrifice his life in vain but for a worthy cause. May God give you the strength and faith to carry on courageously in life. I wish there [were] more appropriate words to write that would lighten the burden of your grief.

May God bless you, and with every best personal wish to you, I remain,
Joseph A. Andrejewski, Capt.
Catholic Chaplain."

★★★★★★★★★★★★★

The Office of the President sent a certificate with the Presidential Seal in full color at the top, the President's bold signature at the bottom, and the following words:

> IN GRATEFUL MEMORY OF PRIVATE FIRST CLASS NICHOLAS L. BONILLA, A. S. NO. 6877454, WHO DIED IN THE SERVICE OF HIS COUNTRY IN THE EUROPEAN AREA, SEPTEMBER 22, 1944.
>
> HE STANDS IN THE UNBROKEN LINE OF PATRIOTS WHO DARED TO DIE THAT FREEDOM MIGHT LIVE AND GROW AND INCREASE ITS BLESSINGS. FREEDOM LIVES AND THROUGH IT, HE LIVES—IN A WAY THAT HUMBLES THE UNDERSTANDING OF MOST MEN.

Ardennes, Battle of the Bulge

On December 16, the men of the 101st, still exhausted from fighting in Holland, began the campaign in the Ardennes Forest in Belgium, the Battle of the

Bulge. Taking Bastogne, the hub for seven highways and one rail line, was critical.

The Nazis sent 25 divisions against 6 Allied divisions, more than 1,000,000 men. An estimated 87 tanks defended the area. Fighting a final defense, German troops surrounded the 10th armored Division and the 101st at Bastogne.

The German commander dispatched a letter to Brigadier General Anthony McAuliffe telling him to surrender within two hours or have his troops completely annihilated. General McAuliffe wrote one word, "Nuts." He wrote the word in large letters, underlined it, put an exclamation point at the end, and sent the message. The German Commander was thoroughly confused until a translator said that the word meant, "Go to hell."

Men of the 101st hoped that General Patton's tanks would break through German lines soon. Troopers fought in the bitter cold with inadequate supplies until January 17, 1945, when the division was relieved.

Four thousand G.I.s were taken prisoner during the Battle of the Bulge. Nazis tried to identify Jewish soldiers and separate them from other prisoners. Some soldiers gave only name, rank, and serial number, but others said they were Jews. Of 350 soldiers sent to Hitler's labor camps, only 80 were really Jews.

Invasion of Germany

General Patton's 3rd Army crossed the Rhine on March 22, 1945, and U. S. troops reached Buchenwald on April 11. They discovered that prisoners had resisted a forced evacuation, thereby saving many lives. Allied air forces reduced Germany's largest cities to rubble. Bombs dropped on Dresden created a firestorm.

On April 12, President Franklin Delano Roosevelt died in Warm Springs, Georgia, and Vice President Harry S. Truman became President of the United States.

By April 23, Soviet troops had reached Berlin, and on April 28, Benito Mussolini and twelve of his former officers were executed. Mussolini's body was returned to Rome where it was hanged upside down on public display. U. S. troops liberated Dachau on April 29. At the concentration camp, American troops found evidence of medical experiments performed on prisoners.

On April 30 in a Berlin bunker, Hitler committed suicide. Heinrich Himmler, head of the Gestapo, who was responsible for the deaths of approximately 11,000,000 civilians, 6,000,000 of them Jews, committed suicide.

Minister of Propaganda Joseph Goebbels watched as an S.S. doctor gave lethal injections to his six children; then an S.S. orderly shot Goebbels and his wife in the head.

Marshal Hermann Goering, commander of the Luftwaffe, surrendered to Allied forces. He was convicted of crimes against humanity at the Nuremburg war crimes trials in 1946. He avoided execution by swallowing a cyanide capsule that he had kept hidden or that had been smuggled to him.

On May 4, the 506th occupied Berchtesgaden, Hitler's Eagle's Nest in the Alps. On May 7, representatives of the German government signed a document of unconditional surrender, and on May 8, 1945, President Truman declared Victory in Europe Day.

On May 9, General Maxwell Taylor announced the surrender to his troops, and the 101st held a memorial service for the men who had died to win the victory.

The End of the War

Marines landed on Iwo Jima on February 19, 1945. Their mission was to capture airfields to use for assault on Japan. Marines fought for 36 days to flush Japanese soldiers from underground bunkers and artillery positions connected by a maze of tunnels. On February 23, the flag of the United States of America was raised on Mt. Suribachi.

On March 9 and 10, 334 B-29s dropped 2,000 tons of firebombs on Tokyo, creating a firestorm and killing approximately 85,000 civilians. Bombing of Japanese cities continued through spring and summer.

On August 6, 1945, Colonel Paul Tibbets and the crew of the B-29 *Enola Gay* dropped an atomic bomb, "Little Boy," on Hiroshima. The city was destroyed, but Japanese armed forces would not surrender. On August 9, Major Charles W. Sweeny piloting a B-29 *Bocks Car* dropped an atomic bomb, "Fat Man," on Nagasaki.

Emperor Hirihito became the first Japanese emperor to speak in public on August 15, 1945. He told his nation that the government and the people would surrender. World War II was over. On September 2, aboard the *U.S.S. Missouri* in Tokyo Bay, General Douglas MacArthur accepted the formal, unconditional surrender of Japan.

The Purple Heart

The Purple Heart Medal was not mailed to Opal until May 1945. The following description was included in the package containing the Purple Heart certificate:

> The Purple Heart was originally established by General George Washington at Newburgh [New York] August 7, 1782 during the war of the Revolution. The Decoration was revived by the War Department on 22 February 1932, the two-hundredth anniversary of General Washington's birth, thus paying respect to his memory and recognizing his military achievements.
>
> The decoration consists of a purple enameled heart within a bronze border on which is mounted in relief a profile head of General Washington in military uniform. Above the enameled heart is the shield of

Washington's coat of arms between two sprays of [laurel] leaves in green enamel. On the reverse below the shield and leaves without enamel is a raised bronze heart with the inscription "For Military Merit," under which is engraved the name of the recipient.

The medal is suspended by a rectangular shaped metal loop with corners rounded from a silk moiré ribbon of purple center and white edges….

J. A. Ulio,
Major General
The Adjutant General
18 May 1945

"Tell Me about My Boy . . ."

In December 1946, Opal received information about options for final burial of Nicky's remains:

"Tell me about my boy" is the request most frequently sent to the quartermaster general of the Army by the next of kin who want additional information on the progress of the War Department's program for the return and final burial of those who died in World War II. The requests are inspired through the fact that the arrangements for carrying out the wishes of the congress which authorizes the place for final disposition must, to use the military term, be phased with the avail-

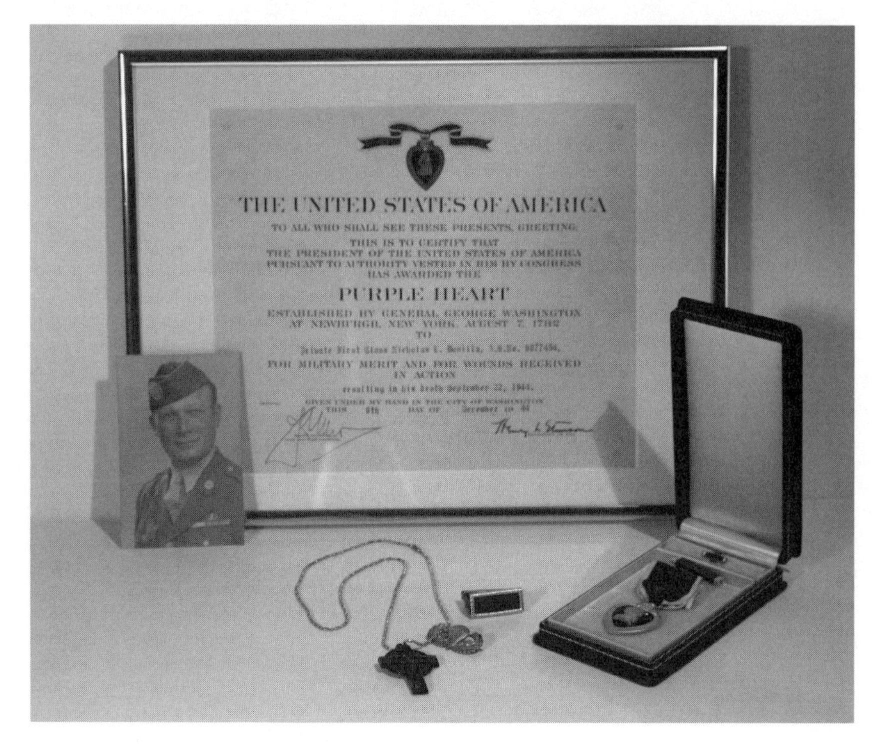

ability of transport to and from overseas, the climatic conditions in many different parts of the world, and the facilities available at home for the production of many items needed in this work. The purpose of this pamphlet is to answer those questions most frequently asked about the program. Of course, it may not answer all questions. If there are further questions about which you are concerned after you have perused this pamphlet, write to The Office of the Quartermaster General, Memorial Division, Washington, 25, DC. You will receive an accurate and prompt reply.

Introduction

World War II brought death to more than 100,000 Americans who were serving their country overseas. While the war was on, most of these honored dead were buried in temporary United States military cemeteries. Some were buried in isolated graves. These latter are being located as fast as possible . . . . Some were lost at sea. Other remains will never be recovered.

Now Congress has passed and the President has signed a bill which authorizes the War Department to take steps to provide a reverent final burial for those who gave the last full measure of devotion. Within the War Department, the Quartermaster Corps is to direct the program, which includes all Army, Navy, Marine, and Coast Guard personnel who died overseas since 3 September, 1939, as well as civilians who were in the service of the United States… for interment in a National Cemetery . . . .

What the Government Plans to Do

The government wants to carry out all feasible wishes of the next of kin. It will carry out these wishes without regard for rank, race, creed, or color…. The relative who has the right to make such a decision may designate the place of burial of the deceased…. If the deceased were married, the surviving spouse has the first and final right.

The Four Options

Next of kin may select one of four options:

1. Remains may be returned to the United States or a possession or territory thereof for interment by the next of kin in a private cemetery.

2. Remains may be returned to a foreign country, the homeland of the deceased or the next of kin for interment in a private cemetery.

3. Remains will be interred in a permanent United States Cemetery overseas.

4. Remains may be returned to the United States for interment in a National Cemetery.

The information herein was compiled by the technical information Branch, Office of the Quartermaster General. Under the supervision of the War Department Public Relations Division.
1 December 1946."

★★★★★★★★★★★★

Opal tried to contact members of Nicky's family in New York to determine their preference for Nicky's final burial, but she was unable to find them.

Opal could have buried Nicky in the Central Church Cemetery at Argo, Alabama. Nicky could have been laid to rest near Clyde, the Keith brother who died as an infant, near Claude, the elder brother who was killed in the coal mine, beside the men who fought in World War I, or beside the men who fought in the 20th Alabama Infantry in the Civil War.

Because Nicky had been dead more than two years, Opal chose to have his body interred in a permanent American Cemetery in Holland. Nicky would continue to repose with the men beside whom he had lived and died.

Nicky at Rest

Nicky and 162 other men of the 502nd were killed or died of wounds in Holland. Many men of the regiment are buried at the Netherlands American Cemetery at Margraten. The cemetery is near the Cologne-Boulogne highway built by the Romans, the highway where Julius Caesar and his legions marched. Soldiers in the armies of Charles V, Napoleon, and Kaiser Wilhelm II also marched along the highway. In May 1940, Hitler's armies invaded the Low Countries using the old Roman route, and in September 1944, Allied troops drove German soldiers from the countries they had occupied for four years. The defeated Nazis retreated along the line of the Cologne-Boulogne highway.

The cemetery is six miles east of Maastricht. The site, gently rolling farmland, was liberated by troops of the 30th Infantry Division on September 13, 1944. The Netherlands American Cemetery, with a Court of Honor, a museum, a 101-foot tower, a bronze statue, and a chapel, was completed and dedicated in 1960.

On the south interior wall of the chapel is the following inscription from a prayer by John Henry Cardinal Newman:

O Lord support us all the day long
Until the shadows lengthen
And the evening comes
And the fever of life is over
And our work is done.
Then in thy mercy

Grant us a safe lodging
And a holy rest and
And peace at the last.

Margraten is the burial place of 8,302 American soldiers. Tablets of the Missing list the names of 1,723 men. Nicky is buried in Plot K, Row 17, Grave 16.

Margraten Cemetery

Epilogue

Opal 1944-2003

After Nicky's death, Opal continued to live with her family. As a widow with one child, she received a pension of $65 a month. The amount was the same for all widows, with an increase of $13 per child up to $100, despite rank or years of service of their husbands. The $10,000 of life insurance Nicky had purchased could not be taken as a lump sum. It was paid in monthly installments of $55.10. According to economic standards of the time, a woman living alone needed an annual income of $1370. For Opal and Sandra, living with John and Louise Keith was an economic and emotional necessity.

In July 1945, Opal began work at Bechtel-McCone Corporation, perhaps hoping to bury her grief in work. She worked as many as sixty hours a week and earned less than a dollar an hour. Louise Keith cared for Sandra.

As a working mother, Opal had little time or energy to see her old friends, but she kept in touch through letters and telephone calls. Roger Gray survived the war and returned to Mary Dean and Scarlett. Despite Mrs. Romeo's early objections, Al Romeo and Evelyn married and raised a family. In 1945, Mrs. Ola Whitten joined the Women's Army Corps. On the third anniversary of the Corps and Mothers Day, May 14, 1945, Pvt. Whitten and seven other mothers serving in the W.A.C.s were honored with a party at Morrison Field in Florida..

Pvt. Whitten's son, Cpl. Wallace Whitten, the father of two children, was killed in the Pacific Theater of Operations later that year. Mrs. Whitten died in 1950. Georgette served in the Women's Marine Corps. She married, but she never had children. Lama also married but had no children. Both Georgette and Lama died of cancer in the 1970s.

When the war plants closed, Opal sold women's clothing in some of Birmingham's best stores. She continued to dress like a "Fifth Avenue model." She was always, as Nicky said, extravagant in her generosity.

In 1946, Fred and Dorothy's husband came home. Fred married Lois Vernon; James married Florence Wallace; and these three couples established new homes

Opal in 1968

and families. Nevertheless, they, along with Pearl, Emmett, and Farris, continued to care for Opal and Sandra.

Opal and Sandra went to catechism classes at St. Paul's Cathedral in Birmingham. Opal said that she had known what the priest taught from the time she was a child, so she did not think it necessary to be instructed.

Several years after Nicky's death, Opal began to go out with a man with whom she had a long-time relationship. However, she never considered marrying again. She said Nicky was the only man she ever loved.

Although Opal worked, she and her mother nursed Sandra through all her childhood injuries and illnesses, including a tonsillectomy and a subsequent hemorrhage.

Opal gave Sandra all the things that other children in Irondale had—roller skates, bicycles, birthstone rings, watches, and portable radios. More importantly, she encouraged Sandra to appreciate good books, history, and music. Opal bought tickets to the Children's Concerts of the Birmingham Symphony Orchestra. She paid for field trips to the Chickamauga Battlefield near Chattanooga, Tennessee, a visit to Mobile, Alabama, to study the history of French settlers, and a visit to Atlanta to see the Civil War Cyclorama. Opal was not involved in P.T.A. and other school related activities, but when Sandra became a cheerleader at Irondale Junior High, Opal bought her daughter a white letter sweater, white tennis shoes, and a blue circular skirt with a white lining.

Florence and James

Opal passed on her fondness for music to Sandra. One Christmas, she gave her daughter an RCA Victor 45 r.p.m. record player. A "free" collection of classical music was part of the package, and Sandra spent hours listening to Beethoven, Chopin, Debussy and Liszt as well as other masters: Little Richard, Bo Diddly, and Fats Domino.

Epilogue

Opal believed, as Nicky did, that Sandra could be "a champ." Opal told Sandra that she was an intelligent girl, that she inherited a good brain from her father. Opal discounted her own intelligence. Although she hated paperwork, she filled out the forms and made the telephone calls necessary to get Sandra approved for G.I. Bill education benefits.

James drove Opal and Sandra to the Veterans Administration Office in Montgomery so that Sandra could take intelligence and aptitude tests. These tests confirmed Sandra's interest in and aptitude for a career in teaching. Opal was proud of her daughter when she enrolled at Jacksonville State University in 1961. When Sandra graduated with a Bachelor's degree in 1964, Opal, Louise Keith, and Sandra's aunts, uncles, and cousins attended the ceremony.

When Opal retired, she cared for her mother and father, cooking and cleaning for them, and loving them. Sandra married and moved away. Louise Keith died peacefully at home at age eighty-eight, and John Keith died two years later.

In 1969, Opal's granddaughter Dena was born. (Her hair is strawberry blond, a tint of Opal's red, and her hazel eyes are just like Nicky's.) Opal (Nanny) helped Sandra care for her family; she cooked, and cleaned and scratched Dena's back as she fell asleep.

In the 1970s, a family friend expressed an interest in dating Opal, but she said, "Oh! No! I wouldn't have any man, not even if he was gold plated!"

With Opal's help, Sandra went to graduate school, and when she was awarded a doctoral degree in 1988, Opal, Dena, James and his wife Florence, Dorothy and Patricia *[Henson]*, and Farris and his wife Sharon *[Murphy]* attended the ceremony.

Opal's health began to decline when she reached age seventy-five. She fell and broke a hip, but she recovered. She had a heart attack, and she recovered. She fell out of a car, the car ran over her leg, and she recovered.

In 1999, Opal fell and broke a shoulder. She had limited use of her left arm; she lost vision in one eye, and was afraid to walk. Opal lived in a nursing home in Birmingham, and her family continued to love and care for her.

On November 16, 2001, the Keith family gathered at the home of Farris and Sharon Hill. Sandra and Farris brought Opal from the nursing home. Dena and her husband Jeff Kemp flew to Birmingham from Colorado with their eight-month old son. When Opal was seated and everyone gathered

Lois and Fred

around her, Dena placed her son in Opal's arms. Dena said, "Nanny, this is Nicholas Scott Kemp." Opal looked into the baby's beautiful blue eyes and said, "Hello, Nicky Boy." On October 12, 2003, Opal met her second great-grandson, Christopher Durham Kemp. On December 1, 2003, Opal died peacefully. Sandra believes that she awoke in Nicky's arms, forever young, forever in love.

Sandra 1944-2003

I grew up in my grandparents' home, and during the war years, it was filled with the aunts, uncles, and cousins about whom you have read. They loved my mother and me and cared for us in every way they could. My grandmother was, as my father said "so good." She was the best person I have ever known, wise and compassionate; my grandfather was feckless but loving. We had no contact with my father's family.

As I grew older, I understood that my life would never be like the lives of other children. I had no father, no brothers, and no sisters. I would not have nieces and nephews unless I married a man with brothers and sisters. My parents were young, intelligent, hopeful, and in love. Perhaps they could have made a happy home and a family to be proud of. However, after my father's death, my mother was emotionally fragile. Sometimes she sat for hours reading my father's letters and examining the mementos of their life together. She seemed to be in another world, a place where I could not go. Even when she was well, she was sad about the unfulfilled promise of our lives.

I am one of approximately 200,000 children who lost a parent in World War II. My mother received veteran's benefits, but there were no counseling programs to help us rebuild our shattered lives. I was afraid to ask my mother about my father, afraid she would become lost in her sorrow. Since my father was buried in Holland, my mother and I attended no funeral; we could not go to see my father's grave.

Sandra in 1968

In the years immediately following, no one talked about the war. People wanted to forget it and get on with living. I do not remember studying WWII in school. I knew more about Henry VIII than I knew about Winston Churchill. (Everybody in the south knew about Franklin D. Roosevelt.)

In elementary school and junior high, I was an average student, willful and undisciplined. No one related my academic and personal lassitude to my father's death and my mother's emotional absence.

I was secretly fascinated with war poetry (Rupert Brooke was one of my favorite poets) and war movies and television shows. I loved *Combat*, and I had a crush on Richard Jaekel. He was short and blond; he looked like pictures of my father. I was angry that Vic Morrow had the starring role when Richard Jaekel was so much better looking.

Like many lonely teenagers, I was angry and resentful. I felt that I did not belong anywhere. I tried to find acceptance in boyfriends, thinking that each one was my true love. Nevertheless, I resented the fact that my mother had a gentleman friend and that she went out with him regularly.

I wanted to get away from home and start a new life, and I did. I went to Jacksonville State University on the G.I. Bill, and I married when I was eighteen. Like many women of my day, I believed that "having" a man was important—a boyfriend, a husband—someone who will fill an emptiness inside.

Although my early marriage failed, I loved learning, and I was a good student. I graduated from college, went to graduate school at Auburn University, and became a college English teacher.

I married again when I was twenty-five years old, but that marriage also failed. I knew no model for a successful marriage. I did not know how real-life husbands and wives were supposed to behave. Even when I was married, I felt isolated. I knew I could go it alone if I had to. I felt that I was the only one I could count on; if something had to be done, I would have to do it.

As a single parent, but with the help of my mother, I raised a daughter and pursued a successful career. Now, I am retired; I have a loving husband, a dear daughter and son-in-law, and precious grandchildren. Until now, I have been afraid of getting lost in the past as I felt my mother had done. Only now do I feel safe enough to know the man and woman who were my parents, free to shed the tears of a lifetime.

In 2001, I joined the American Orphans of World War II Network founded by Anne Bennett Mix, and I am in contact with approximately 750 orphans and their families who live all over America. They are the brothers and sister I never had, and they are helping me to know my father, my mother, and my self.

Meeting my mother as a young woman full of hope, and finding the father whom I knew only as a faded photograph, I have learned to appreciate the heroism and humanity of my parents and a generation of men and women like them.

My mother loved my father with all her heart and soul. She thought he was so good a soldier that he would survive the war. But she accepted his death with dignity, and she met her responsibilities to the best of her abilities.

My father believed he was one of the best soldiers in the world, and he believed that freedom was worth dying for. He believed that our country's leaders were great men, and that the Allies would win the war. He was confident, perhaps even cocky. He had a dogface's disdain for Army rules and regulations. He drank his share at the Town Pump. Even though he was from New York City, he could drive a car. He claimed to be a good cook. He liked to swim and play baseball. He took great care to boost my mother's morale even as he suffered the brutality of combat.

For his country, he gave everything he had-family, friends, fortune, comfort, health, and life. He carried a lock of my hair in his wallet, and he wore my baby shoes around his neck. Although he never met me, he loved me.

My longing has been fulfilled; my hope has been realized. My father has come home to me, and I can say, "Daddy, I love you."

Notes

Some quotations in the text come from original documents collected and preserved by Opal Keith Bonilla but not identified by publisher or date of publication. Quotations from news stories are identified in the text with the names of newspapers, titles of articles, and names of writers and date of publication, if available. Facts about the 502nd Parachute Regiment and the 101st Airborne Division are found in many sources, primarily those listed in the Bibliography. Quotations in the text are from the following sources:

1. Franklin Delano Roosevelt, "The Annual Message to Congress delivered by President Franklin D. Roosevelt on January 6, 1942," White House news release on www.ibiblio.org/pha/policy/1942/html.

2. Jerry Autry, *General William C. Lee: Father of the Airborne* (San Francisco: Airborne Press, 1995), 110.

3. Autry, *General William C. Lee*, 130.

4. Cesare Almaggi and Alfredo Pallavisini, *2194 Days of War: An Illustrated Chronology of the Second World War*, (New York: Barnes and Noble, 1977), 305.

5. Doris Weatherford, *American Women in World War II.* (New York: Facts on File, 1990), 250, quoting Henry A. Bowman. "Should Soldiers Marry?" *American Magazine*, (August 1942), 74.

6. Weatherford, *Women in World War II*, 281, quoting Jonathan Wake, "The Censor Reads Your Letters," *Good Housekeeping* (November 1942), 117.

7. Robert M. Bowen, *Fighting with the Screaming Eagles: With the 101st Airborne Division from Normandy to Bastogne*, (Stackpole, PA: Green Hill Books, 2001), 27, 249.

8. John Keegan, *Six Armies in Normandy: From D-Day to the Liberation of Paris*, (New York: Penguin books, 1983), 11-12.

9. Dale P. Harper, "Axis Sally," *World War II Magazine*, http://womenshistory.about.com.

10. Stephen E. Ambrose, *The Victors: Eisenhower and his Boys: The Men of World War II*. (New York: Simon & Schuster, 1998), 79, 80.

11. Anne Frank, *The Diary of Anne Frank: The Definitive Edition* Otto Frank, Ed. Mirjam Pressler, Ed., Susan Masotty, Tran. (New York: Doubleday, 2001), 311-323.

12. Diane Burke Fessler, Ed. *No Time for Fear: Voices of American Military Nurses in World War II*. (East Lansing, MI: Michigan State University Press, 1996), 167, 168.

13. Marianne Moore, "Keeping Their World Large" *Poets of World War II*. Ed. Harvey Shapiro. (American Poets Project: Literary Classics of the United States 2003), 16.

14. Louis Simpson, "Carentan O Carentan," *Poets of World War II*.183-185.

15. Leonard Rapport and Arthur Norwood Jr., *Rendezvous with Destiny*, (Old Saybrook, CT: Konecky & Konecky, 1948), 177-190.

16. Mark Bando, *The 101st Airborne: The Screaming Eagles at Normandy*, (Osceola, WI: MBI Publishing Company), 2001, 101-119.

17. John M. Taylor, *An American Soldier: The Wars of General Maxwell Taylor*, (Novato, CA: Presidio Press, 2001), 92, quoting Rapport and Norwood, Rendezvous With Destiny, 249.

18. S.L.A. Marshall. *Men Against Fire: The Problem of Battle Command in Future War*. (Gloucester, MA: Peter Smith), 1978. 180.

19. Rapport and Norwood. *Rendezvous with Destiny*, 293-298. See also Donald R. Burgett, *The Road to Arnhem: a Screaming Eagle in Holland*, (New York: Dell Publishing Co, 2001), 109, 110.

Bibliography

Some facts and numbers in the sources listed below are in disagreement. Such disagreement may occur because previously secret documents have been released, recent research has produced new information, and personal recollections tend to vary. Because the number of books about the 101st Airborne Division is vast, only the standard references or those more recently published are included here.

Ambrose, Stephen E. *Band of Brothers: E Company, 506th Regiment, 101st Airborne from Normandy to Hitler's Eagle's Nest*. New York: Simon & Schuster, 1992.

——————*D-Day June 6, 1944: The Climactic Battle of World War II*. New York: Touchstone Books, 1995

——————*The Victors: Eisenhower and His Boys: The Men of World War II*. New York: Simon and Schuster, 1998.

Autry, Jerry. *General William C. Lee: Father of the Airborne*. San Francisco: Airborne Press, 1995.

Badsey, Stephen. *Arnhem 1944*. London: Osprey Publishing Limited, 1993.

—————— *Normandy 1944*. London: Osprey, Publishing Limited, 1990.

Baker, George. *The Sad Sack*. New York: Henry Holt and Company, 1945.

Bando, Mark. *The 101st Airborne Division: The Screaming Eagles at Normandy*. Osceola, Wisconsin: MBI Publishing Company, 2001.

———— *Vanguard of the Crusade: The 101st Airborne Division in World War II.* Bedford, PA: Aberjona Press, 2003.

Bowen, Robert M. *Fighting With the Screaming Eagles: With the 101st Airborne from Normandy to Bastogne.* London: Greenhill Books, 2001.

Burgett, Donald. *Curahee: A Screaming Eagle at Normandy*. Novato, California: Presidio Press, 1999.

———— *The Road to Arnhem: A Screaming Eagle in Holland*. Novato, California: Presidio Press, rpt. Dell Publishing, 2001.

————*Seven Roads to Hell: a Screaming Eagle at Bastogne*. Novato, California: Presidio Press, 1999, rpt. Dell Publishing, 2000.

Colley, David. *The Road to Victory: The Untold Story of World War II's Red Ball Express*. New York: Warner Books, Inc., 2000.

Fessler, Diane Burke. Ed. *No Time for Fear: Voices of American Military Nurses in World War II.* East Lansing, Michigan: Michigan State University Press, 1996.

Frank, Anne. *The Diary of Anne Frank: Definitive Edition*. Ed. Otto Frank, Ed. Mirjam Pressler, Trans. Susan Massotty. New York: Doubleday, 2001.

Hadler, Susan Johnson, Ann Bennett Mix, and Calvin L.Christman. *Lost in the Victory: Reflections of American War Orphans of World War II*. Denton, Texas: University of North Texas Press, 1998.

Harrison, George A. *Cross Channel Attack.* Old Saybrook, Connecticut: Konecky & Konecky, 1950.

Keegan, John. *Six Armies in Normandy: From D-Day to the Liberation of Paris.* New York: Penguin Books, 1983.

Koskimaki, George. *D-Day with the Screaming Eagles*. Madelia, MN, 1970. Reprinted by Casemate Publishing Company, Havertown, PA, 2002.

————*Hell's Highway: Chronicle of the 101st Airborne Division in the Holland Campaign, September- November 1944*. Havertown, PA: Casemate, 2003.

Bibliography

Litoff, Judy Barrett, and David C. Smith, Eds., *Since You Went Away: World War II Letters from American Women on the Home Front*. Lawrence, Kansas: University Press of Kansas, 1991.

Marshall, S.L A. *Men Against Fire: The Problem of Battle Command in Future War*. Gloucester, MA: Peter Smith, 1978.

Mauldin, Bill. *Up Front.* New York: Henry Holt and Company, 1945.

McRae, Bennie J. Jr. "The Negro Pilot Training Program." United States Air Force History and Archives, Maxwell Air Force Base, Alabama, at www.coax.net.

Moore, Brenda L. *To Serve My Country, To Serve My Race*. New York: New York University Press, 1996.

O'Donnell, Patrick K. *Beyond Valor: World War II's Rangers and Airborne Veterans Reveal the Heart of Combat*. New York: Touchstone Books, 2001.

Powell, Geoffrey. *The Devil's Birthday: The Bridges to Arnhem 1944*. London: Buchan & Enright, Publishers, 1984.

Rappoport, Leonard, and Arthur Norwood, Jr. *Rendezvous with Destiny*, Old Saybrook, Connecticut: Konecky& Konecky, 1948.

Roosevelt, Franklin D. "The Annual Message to Congress delivered by President Franklin D. Roosevelt on January 6, 1942," White House news release, www.ibiblio.org/pha/policy/1942/html.

Ryan, Cornelius. *The Longest Day*. New York: Touchstone, 1994.

——————*A Bridge Too Far*. New York: Simon and Schuster, 1974.

Almagggi, Cesare, and Alfredo Pallavivini. *2194 Days of War: An Illustrated Chronology of the Second World War*. New York: Barnes and Noble, 1977.

Shapiro, Harvey, Ed. *Poets of World War II*. American Poets Project, The Library of America, 2003.

Tuttle, William M. Jr. "Daddy's Gone to War": *The Second World War in the Lives of American Children*. New York: Oxford University Press, 1993.

Warren, John C. *Airborne Operations in World War II, European Theater*, U.S.A.F. Historical Studies: No. 97. Manhattan, Kansas: Sunflower University Press, 1956.

Weatherford, Doris. *American Women in World War II*. New York: Facts on File, 1990.